Selections
A HISTORY OF BRITISH
BIRDS
by Thomas
BEWICK

with a
new introduction by
Michael Marqusee

PADDINGTON
Masterpieces of the
Illustrated Book

Library of Congress Cataloging in Publication Data

Bewick, Thomas, 1753-1828.
  Selections from A history of British birds.

  (Masterpieces of the illustrated book)
  1. Birds—Great Britain 2. Birds—Great Britain—Pictorial Works. I. Title
QL690. G7B52 1976   598.2'941   76-4456
ISBN 0-8467-0144-8

© Paddington Press 1976

Published by Paddington Press Ltd., New York and London
Printed in England by Balding & Mansell Ltd., Wisbech, Cambs.

CONTENTS

Land Birds

Introduction by Michael Marqusee	5	The Black Woodpecker	105
Preface to the sixth edition	17	The Nuthatch	107
Preface to the original (1797) edition	21	The Grosbeak	109
Introduction to the original edition	25	The Yellow Bunting	111
Explanation of Technical Terms	48	The Tawny Bunting	113
		Of the Finch	115
The Golden Eagle	55	The Goldfinch	116
The Osprey	57	The Linnet	118
Peregrine Falcon	59	The Spotted Flycatcher	120
The Kite	61	The Lark	122
The Ash Coloured Falcon	63	The Woodlark	125
The Hobby	65	The Grey Wagtail	127
The Sparrowhawk	67	*Of the Warblers*	128
Stone Falcon	69	The Redbreast	129
The Merlin	71	The Passerine Warbler	133
The Eagle-Owl	73	The Reed Warbler	134
The Long-Eared Owl	75	The Black-Cap	135
The Female Short-Eared Owl	77	The Yellow Wren	137
Of the Shrike	78	The Wren	139
The Ash-Coloured Shrike	80	The Crested Titmouse	141
The Crow	82	The Marsh Titmouse	143
The Rook	84	The Cock	144
The Jack-Daw	87	The Pheasant	149
The Magpie	90	The Peacock	153
The Jay	91	The Partridge	157
The Chatterer	94	The Quail	160
The Starling	96	The Great Bustard	163
The Redwing	99	The Great Plover	167
The Blackbird	101	The Golden Plover	170
The Ring Ouzel	103	The Sanderling	172

Water Birds

Preface	175	The Common Gallinule	255
Introduction	179	The Great-Crested Grebe	258
		The Dusky Grebe	260
The Heron	191	The Lesser Guillemot	262
The Night Heron	195	The Lesser Imber	264
The Little Egret	197	The Sandwich Tern	265
The Bittern	199	The Roseate Tern	267
The Little Bittern	202	The Black-Backed Gull	269
The Spoonbill	204	The Dun-Diver	271
Of the Ibis	207	The Red-Breasted Merganser	276
The Curlew	208	The Smew	278
The Woodcock	210	The Mute Swan	280
The Snipe	216	The Swan Goose	284
The Judcock	220	The Tame Goose	286
The Godwit	222	The White-Fronted Wild Goose	293
Of the Sandpiper	224	The Eider Duck	295
The Lapwing	225	The Musk Duck	300
The Green Sandpiper	229	The Scoter	303
The Knot	231	The Tame Duck	306
The Red-Legged Sandpiper	233	The Gadwall	310
The Purre	236	The Pochard	312
The Little Stint	239	The Pintail Duck	315
The Turnstone	240	The Tufted Duck	318
The Turnstone	242	The Teal	320
Of the Avoset	244	The Shag	323
The Water Ouzel	245	The Gannet	326
The Kingfisher	250	The Scolopax Sabini	332
The Water Rail	252	The Selninger Sandpiper	334

INTRODUCTION

Perhaps no artist is more commonly associated with the artistic representation of birds than John James Audubon. In 1827, some years before the publication of his enormously successful *Birds of America*, Audubon paid a visit to Thomas Bewick at his home in Newcastle. He described the encounter in his *Ornithological Biography:* "He was a tall stout man, with a large head, and with eyes placed farther apart than those of any man I have ever seen: a perfect old English man, full of life, although seventy-four years of age, active and prompt in his labors." A year before their meeting Bewick had supervised the publication of his final version (selections from which are reproduced here) of the two-volume *History of British Birds*. It was as the compiler and illustrator of this book that Audubon had sought out the old man, and today it stands unquestionably as his single most important achievement, worthy of the homage paid to it by the young American.

Thomas Bewick was, more than anything else, a master of the illustrated book. And in devoting himself to ornithological illustration, he was responding to two of the needs in which the illustrated book originates. For in making images of birds, he was, with each mark on the page, purveying both scientific information and visual beauty.

Perhaps the earliest representations of birds to combine elegance and accuracy were the drawings made by Pisanello in the early fifteenth century. In fact, the Renaissance of which Pisanello is a harbinger is equally a chapter in the history of science and the history or art. Study of the Renaissance raises many questions, but one of its undeniable achievements was the introduction of new ways of representing the reality that both scientists and artists were learning to observe. The focus of their researches was the human body, the theme of Leonardo's dissections and drawings which constitute the most remarkable joint venture of science and art. These drawings show the structure and function of the body more clearly than any photograph. This is also true, though in a less spectacular fashion, of Bewick's *Birds*. Even today, few ornithology manuals are illustrated with photographs; the process of selection, clarification, and definition which science requires is also the *criterion*, the critical element, in art. It is therefore not surprising that the history of the illustrated book should be closely allied to the history of scientific ideas and information.

Bewick's *British Birds* could not have been conceived without the development, in the preceding century, of systems for classifying natural phenomena. Carl Linnaeus is the preeminent name in this field, but for Bewick the important figure was George Louis Leclerc de Buffon, who issued the many volumes of his *Histoire Naturelle* between 1749 and 1788. He is cited throughout Bewick's work as an inspiration and authority. The printed book, particularly the illustrated book, was the natural vehicle for the investigations of Linnaeus and Buffon. For there is a correspondence between the biological divisions of kingdom, phylum, genus and species, and those of volume, chapter, and paragraph. Is it not possible that, in their attempt to give shape to their new knowledge of nature, the eighteenth-century scientists were influenced by the structure of books, which had embodied and preserved all of man's previous knowledge? In a strange way, Bewick's book is not as removed as may seem from the medieval bestiaries which contain some of the earliest images of birds in Western art. Only with Bewick it is not the single image but the whole book, in its implied equivalence to the natural world, that has assumed symbolic value.

The presence of illustrations in these books derives not only from the need for visual data, but also from the assumption that the natural created world is beautiful. The object of the scientist's study of nature had been, in Bewick's words, "to trace the Author of nature through his works," and these works, having been designed by the supreme artist, had all the attractions of a work of art—order, inventiveness, variety. For Buffon, this was probably a convenient rationalization of a desire to study nature for what we would call today purely scientific reasons. For Bewick, it was a way of formulating what we would call today a deep emotional response to nature. In this respect the Bird books fed another apetite which had been growing throughout the century. It can be found in the poetry of James Thomson, another celebrator of "the plumy race, the tenants of the sky," whom Bewick admired and illustrated. There is no place here to discuss when and why this poetical view of nature appeared, but one can safely say that it gained wide currency in the eighteenth century, and that the conservationism and nature-worship of our own time, even our fondness for Bewick, are a continuation of these eighteenth-century trends. In Bewick's art, this feeling cannot yet justly be called Romantic. A true

6

Romantic, such as Wordsworth, born a generation after Bewick, emphasized the alienation of mind from nature as much as their affinity. And as a corollary of this alienation, he insisted that the scientist (who "murders to dissect") and the artist look at nature in fundamentally different ways. Bewick does not participate in this divorce of science from art; as I have tried to explain, the entire enterprise of these volumes, with their easy mingling of narrative vignettes and fact-dispensing prose, assumes a harmony of science, nature, and art.

Bewick does resemble Wordsworth, however, in that his love of natural surroundings can be traced back to his childhood, which he spent on a farm in the Tyne valley. The first chapters of his *Memoir* (a superb new edition of which has recently been published by Oxford University Press, with a biographical introduction by Iain Bain) show how profound and enduring were the impressions of that childhood. He recounts not only his early treks through woods and fields, but also his encounters with local characters – retired soldiers and seamen (see the vignette on the first contents page), workmen and preachers, the various types celebrated and mourned in Goldsmith's *The Deserted Village*, a poem from which Bewick often quoted. From his own account he appears to have been a vigorous and mischievous child, delighting in odd whims and practical jokes. These he recalls, at the end of his life, with fondness and humor; but he also recalls, and with equal emotion the reprimands he received from his father and from the local vicar, who was his first teacher. Their homiletic method, and their habit of bolstering discipline by invoking the grave, were as important in shaping Bewick's art as his solitary rambles through the wilder parts of the countryside. Together, these two childhood experiences became the source material for the little vignettes – perhaps the chief attraction of his works – which Bewick called *tale*-pieces. In these scenes wit and solemnity are never far apart; indeed, in something like the cut on p. 62, they are indistinguishable.

In examining an artist's life it is often easy to locate the source of the subject matter of his art, but more difficult to say why he should ever have thought of turning this matter into art. Very early Bewick found he needed to "give vent to this propensity of figuring whatever I had seen – at that time I had never heard the word 'drawing' being made use of, nor did I know of any other paintings, besides the Kings Arms in the Church, and the signs in Ovingham of the Black Bull, the White Horse, the Salmon and the Hounds and Hare." He drew at first with bits of chalk on brick or slate; later he was given pencils and paper. Because he received no formal instruction in art, he was forced to develop his own methods for representing depth, movement, tone, etc. "Of patterns or drawings I had none – the Beasts & Birds which enlivened the beautiful scenery of my native Hamlet furnished me with an endless supply of subjects." In this way Bewick grew up along with his art. Bearing this in mind, one can understand the homogeneity of his subject and style, and also the failings of his art on the rare occasions when he ventured outside his special field.

Bewick's parents and his beloved vicar encouraged the boy's "propensity of figuring" without any of the pretense or ambition so often associated with parental encouragement of the arts. For them, as for Bewick himself, it was just another skill. Accordingly, he was apprenticed at the age of fourteen to Ralph Beilby, a Newcastle artisan who made clock faces, coffin plates, trade cards, settings for jewels and watches, and other items required by the local middle classes. In the course of his seven-year apprenticeship Bewick acquired almost all of these skills, most of which were based on copper-plate engraving. The fitful ruptures between artist and public, by then a regular feature of artictic life in the remote centers of London and Paris, did not disturb the working routines of a provincial craftsman like Beilby. In his shop commerce dictated aesthetics. It would be wrong, however, to think that the tradition to which Bewick was apprenticed was crass in its subordination of beauty to utility. Anyone who has poured tea from an elegant old teapot, or stored trinkets in an ornamented box, knows the pleasure of discovering a modest beauty in the midst of the necessary affairs of life. When such objects were the manufacture of a neighbor or acquaintance, the pleasure must have been that much more intimate. Because these things were not set apart from the intercourse of daily life they embellished it in a way that self-professed works of art, for all that they teach and give the inner life, do not. We can see the ramifications of this tradition in Bewick's devotion to the illustrated book. For the art of illustration is found not on a museum wall, but in a book which one can live with and open at leisure.

Bewick's reputation as the father of wood engraving, widespread in his own time, persists to this day. Few technical developments in the history of art have been so consistently linked with a single name. Thomas Bewick is not, however, the inventor of wood engraving. His *Memoir* is virtually silent on this subject, but we know that end-grain woodblocks were used by printers at least a century before Bewick's first experiments in the medium. Nonetheless, Bewick was the first to demonstrate its artistic capacity and, especially, its suitability for illustrating printed books.

Like engraving and etching, wood engraving was derived from the simple manipulation of processes already in use. Woodcuts, which began to appear in the early fifteenth century, are made on a plank of soft wood cut so that the grain runs parallel to the surface. The artist uses a knife to remove the spaces that are to appear white (blank) in the final print. This is the method used in the great works of Dürer and Holbein. Because the grain of the wood inhibits the movement of the knife, making it difficult to produce a fine or flexible line, the woodcut was gradually replaced in book illustration by the intaglio processes of engraving and etching. Wood engraving differs from wood cutting in several ways, and has several advantages over engraving and etching as a medium for illustration. First, it is a relief process, and can therefore be printed along with moveable type. Second, the wood (usually boxwood) is much harder; when properly treated, it can be as durable as steel. Third, the wood is cut across the grain, so that the annual rings are visible, and the artist cuts away the white spaces with a fine-pointed engraver's burin. Thus the grain no longer inhibits the movement of the artist's hand, enabling him to produce a finer, more flexible line. (The hardness and density of the end-grain, however, makes the process a laborious one, as Audubon reports: "Bewick began to shew me, as he laughingly said, how easy it was to cut wood; but I soon saw that cutting wood in his style and manner was no joke, although to him indeed it seemed easy.")

Bewick's example established wood engraving as the preeminent method of illustration until the end of the nineteenth century. Newspapers, magazines, fine illustrated books and technical manuals, original compositions and routine reproductive work – wood engraving was used for all of these. Much of Daumier's work, almost all of Doré's and Menzel's, not to mention a host of English illustrators, was executed on wood. In this respect Bewick's influence can hardly be exaggerated. Many of the apprentices trained in his Newcastle shop went on to highly successful careers in the London publishing world. Some, like Luke Clennell and John Jackson, produced pieces of virtuoso engraving which even Bewick himself never attempted. But no artist ever quite returned to Bewick's own characteristic way of handling the block. There is a sense in which, for all their virtuosity, none of them exploited the nature of the wood engraving as he did. Bewick was famous for his use of white line technique, in which the design is conceived as a system of white lines or blank spaces cut out of the surface of the block. Bewick adopts this manner in the foliage and generally in the backgrounds of the vignettes. But his *schemata* are not always that simple; he often moves back and forth between white line and black line, flicking out patches of white or leaving in discs or streaks of black, using all the strategies at the wood engraver's command to achieve tonal variety, and it is through this variety that he organizes the design.

I confess that I have not found in Bewick's work the fluency or ease of execution for which he is often praised. He was a tireless and ingenious craftsman (Audubon noted "his delicate and beautiful tools. . . all made by himself") but the craft he practiced was refractory one. His cuts are clean and economical, but they are not tossed off, quickly and automatically. He was an effective but not a facile draughtsman, and his preparatory drawings indicated only the general placement of the figures in the composition. As he engraved, he had to rethink the entire design according to the peculiar black-and-white properties of wood engraving. Such rethinking required much detailed, eye-straining labor. This should be borne in mind when we examine his results; otherwise, we will search in vain for elegance or

9

technical sophistication that simply is not there, and which, indeed, would be out of place in Bewick's art.

Bewick's first wood engravings, executed during his apprenticeship, appeared in an edition of *Gay's Fables* (1776), and for one of these he won a premium from the Society for the Encouragement of Arts. After leaving Beilby's shop he returned to his native village of Cherryburn, where he remained for two quiet years. In 1776 he wandered through Scotland on foot (one of the most exuberant chapters of the *Memoir* is devoted to this journey) then worked for several months in London. He detested the metropolis and returned to Newcastle in 1777 to set up in partnership with Ralph Beilby, his former master. In 1784 some of his wood engravings appeared in an edition of *Select Fables*, along with others by his younger brother John, now serving as his apprentice.

Shortly after the death of his mother and father in 1785 he conceived and began work on his first major book, the *General History of Quadrupeds*. In addition to the many attentively studied and patiently cut figures of quadrupeds, Bewick introduced his own adaptation of the ancient tradition of the vignette, his famous *tale*-pieces. Inserted strategically within the prose text, these miniature scenes provide an excellent visual balance as well as a kind of light relief. On its first appearance in 1790, the book was an outstanding commercial success, running through four editions in ten years. Bewick had managed to combine both the sentimental and scientific interest in nature within the harmonious format of the illustrated book.

The success of the *Quadrupeds*, the extent of which Bewick himself could never have expected, led him to undertake the *History of British Birds* in the following year. A revealing passage in the *Memoir* recounts his conception of the book. After listing over a dozen bird books with which he was already familiar, and paying them homage as his exemplars, he asserts that: "at the beginning of this undertaking I made up my mind to copy nothing from the works of others but to stick to nature as closely as I could." He spent two months in 1791 in the Wycliffe Museum, making studies from the large collection of stuffed specimens. He found, however, that sticking to nature was more difficult than it seemed. Noting "the very great difference between preserved specimens and those from nature," particularly in the arrangement of the feathers and the carriage of the spine, he decided to draw only from freshly shot or live animals, and occupied himself in the meantime by creating a new set of tail-pieces. In the preparatory sketches of the birds (most of which are now in the British Museum and the Natural History Museum of Newcastle), Bewick first delineated the basic shape and posture of the bird and then applied watercolor as a rough guide to the arrangement and coloring of the plumage. Bewick's strong pencil line, not delicate or refined but somehow resilient and convincing, always searches out the essentials. His manner of posing the birds in a natural setting is not as spectacular as Audubon's but he always contrives to reveal just the right amount of information about the shape and structure of the bird. He shows us what we need to know and no more.

Although in cutting his wood blocks Bewick adhered closely to the overall design of his original sketches, the coloring is treated freely and the backgrounds are generally improvised. To see Bewick's imagination at work, choose almost any of the birds and examine a small portion of his cutting in detail. Though forced to represent all manner of color and texture through the simple alternation of blacks and whites, he hardly ever repeats himself. Only by such close examination can one form any idea of the scope of Bewick's labor. In a letter to a friend, he reports that he personally cut all but six of the birds, and it is fair to assume that the same is true of a majority of the tail-pieces. The hours of eye-strain did not go unrewarded. In 1797 the first volume of the *Birds* appeared and was an even greater success than the *Quadrupeds*. Beilby, who had written most of the text of this volume, could not agree with Bewick on the distribution of credit on the title-page and their partnership was dissolved shortly thereafter. Bewick wrote all of the second volume, which appeared in 1804, and continued to revise and supplement both volumes in the many succeeding editions.

Some of the tail-pieces in the *Water Birds* have traditionally been attributed to Luke Clennell. Clennell was one of the most talented of Bewick's apprentices ("of distinguished ability, both as a draughtsman and wood engraver," said Bewick) and pursued a successful career as an illustrator in London for a decade before going insane in 1817. His excellent and rare water colors are now highly valued.

The success of the *Birds* and *Quadrupeds* made Bewick into something of a celebrity, receiving visits from strangers like Audubon and requests for illustrations from London publishers. Nonetheless, he maintained his old workshop in Newcastle and continued to take on apprentices and commissions for copper-plate engraving. Aside from his own productions, he contributed illustrations to a number of other books, including editions of the poetry of Thomson and Burns. The most important of these books is the *Poems of Goldsmith and Parnell* of 1795, published by Bewick's old friend William Bulmer through his Shakespeare Printing Office. This volume is still considered to be one of the finest specimens of English book design. Unfortunately, Bewick felt that he had not received fair compensation for his contribution to the book and accepted no more commissions for Bulmer's press. The only other volume of typographic beauty containing Bewick illustrations is his own *Aesop's Fables* of 1818.

Bewick spent the last years of his life writing the *Memoir* and cutting a few tail-pieces for a book of British Fishes, which he never completed. At this time his name was already being used to sell books with which he had no connection. His reputation had spread to Europe and America, where Alexander Anderson issued an imitation of the *Quadrupeds* in 1794. Articles on his life and work had appeared in London journals and people were collecting his books, blocks, and sketches. The Bewick cult had already gathered many adherents by the time of his death in 1828.

This cult, which was to thrive throughout the nineteenth century (producing some noteworthy bibliographical extravagances), and which lingers still among antiquarians and bibliophiles, has probably done Bewick's art more harm than good. Any exaggerated account of Bewick's merits can lead only to disappointment with his actual achievement; it is so easy to drown the minor artist in words. In dealing with one such as Bewick we should try to distinguish the appeal of his art from the appeal of the extraneous elements associated with that art. In Bewick's case, that means his appeal as a modest North Country craftsman with an engaging personality, a representative of the unspoiled pre-industrial world whose work recalls, in Collins' words,

. . . . some gentle song
Of those whose lives are yet sincere and plain.

We must make this distinction, not so that we can reject one aspect of the artist in favor of another, but so that we have no illusions about what it is that we enjoy in a particular artist's work. The unwillingness to make this distinction is a trivialization of art, a "pretense of art to destroy art" as Blake said.

Still, making such a distinction is easier said than done: to define an artist's genius is always a perilous affair. To begin with, Bewick's subject matter, for which we all cherish a sentimental affection, is not extraneous to his art. In a special sense, it *is* his art. His canny way of choosing scenes, of admitting the viewer at a certain moment and from a certain angle, is one of his chief accomplishments. A man walking through the snow on stilts, a fox peering into a hunter's trap, a beggar fending off a dog, no one but Bewick would have thought to show us these events. On p. 72 a man drinks water from the crown of his hat while a motto cut into a nearby rock proclaims "Grata Sum": how simple! how common! yet how far from cliché. We wonder that we had never before thought of this as a subject for art. This simple presentation of the familiar but not quite ordinary could be illustrated by dozens of examples.

Look at the strange cut on p. 115, showing rather commonplace demons distracting and frustrating the susceptible country-folk. Here Bewick seems to have tapped some real vein of popular culture. Look again, at his portrayal of the results of overindulgence (p. 270), or his *vanitas*, with its contrast of old age and buoyant youth, or his image of the blind man guided by the lame man whom he carries on his back. In these creations proverbial wisdom seems to have found an appropriate visual expression, emblematically concise yet retaining the lively, casual, anecdotal style which is one of its principal attractions. Bewick maintained just the right distance from popular culture. He grew up in it, never abandoned it altogether, and lavished much affection on it. In the *Memoir* he records his interest in the superstitions of the border districts, and his love of old ballads and bagpipe music. One of his cherished personal projects was to revive the popular single-sheet woodcuts he had seen hanging on the walls of country cottages in his youth. But Bewick taught himself enough so that he was no longer actually part of that culture. He made use of it in his art, but he did not sentimentalize or accept it uncritically.

Bewick must have known that this was his strength, for he returned again and again to the world of his youth, with its inexhaustible supply of incident: men blowing up fires, digging graves, fording streams. Bewick created in these scenes a peculiarly English form of pastoral, full of awkward moments, bad weather, farmyard violence, and no trace of Virgilian sunniness. Its source was in his great store of childhood memories. Indeed, it is because he had to scrounge through his memory to find these scenes that Bewick was able so often to choose just the right moment, the intriguing moment, to represent. "Perhaps few have passed through life," he notes, "without experiencing the pleasure that a retrospect of the times past thus affords to old cronies, in talking over the recollections of youthful frolics and even the discipline which followed in consequence of them." Bewick does not filter these recollections through a veil of nostalgic regret. When he shows us a group of boys flying a kite or blowing a toy sail boat with a billows, it is a sense of the liveliness of the past, and not merely its loss, that animates his burin. There are no idle tears in Bewick's work.

Bewick is not a great painter of natural surfaces. There is little attempt to render details of plants and trees, either in the engravings or the drawings. In his representation of foliage and fields the same configurations of engraver's marks appear again and again. What inspires Bewick's best blocks is a more general response to the phenomena of nature. In the rain-streaked tail-piece on p. 223, a man is found huddled against a sheltering tree. We see clearly that he is seeking protection from the cold and wet, and by presenting him from behind and from a slight distance, Bewick gives us a full view of the over-arching tree and the engulfing storm. This block moves us by its evocation of the greater realities of wind and rain; it is another example of Bewick's North Country preoccupation with foul weather and early death, which pervades both volumes of the *Birds*. His horses standing stoically in the rain, his travelers peering at signposts in the dark, the half-toppled stone with its motto "Good times and bad times and all times get over"–these are reminders, without bitterness or irony, of nature's domination over man. It is a great but homely truth, encountered casually, as it were, by the way.

Nonetheless, Bewick never allowed the wildness and turbulence of his natural settings to overawe him. His style does not partake of the storm it portrays. His grasp of essentials–that knowledge of just how much should be cut away to make a figure or scene comprehensible–hardly ever fails him. We can observe this in the excellent cut on p. 119, showing a man stretched out on the ground with the date "June, 1795" inscribed in the bushes next to him. An odd place to find a man in this position: has he fallen asleep by the roadside? Bewick's treatment of the figure is loose and simple. If the character had been any more elaborate the scene would have been drained of its curious emptiness. The bushes are barely indicated; there is a hint of distance. Such is Bewick's grasp of artistic economy. It allows his best compositions, like the one at the bottom of this page, with its balletic balancing of tiny figures skating on a frozen pond, to float, unframed, anywhere on the white page. Few other styles have been so profitably confined within the bound pages of the illustrated book.

Michael Marqusee

A
HISTORY
OF
BRITISH BIRDS.

BY

THOMAS BEWICK.

VOL. I.

CONTAINING THE

HISTORY AND DESCRIPTION OF

LAND BIRDS.

NEWCASTLE:

PRINTED BY EDW. WALKER, PILGRIM-STREET,

FOR T. BEWICK: SOLD BY HIM, LONGMAN AND CO. LONDON;

AND ALL BOOKSELLERS.

1826.

PREFACE

TO THE SIXTH EDITION.

—

WHEN I first undertook my labours in Natural History, my strongest motive was to lead the minds of youth to the study of that delightful pursuit, the surest foundation on which Religion and Morality can efficiently be implanted in the heart, as being the unerring and unalterable book of the Deity. My writings were intended chiefly for youth; and the more readily to allure their pliable, though discursive, attention to the Great Truths of Creation, I illustrated them by figures delineated with all the fidelity and animation I was able to impart to mere wood-cuts without colour; and as instruction is of little avail without constant cheerfulness and occasional amusement, I interspersed the more serious studies with *Tale*-pieces of gaiety and humour; yet even in these seldom without an endeavour to illustrate some truth, or point some moral; so uniting with my ardent wish to improve the rising generation, the exercise of my art and profession, by which I lived. Little was I then aware that children of a larger growth, and even minds illumined with talent, and hearts warmed with liberality, would have caught from my exertions a kindred feeling, and extended the popularity of my labours farther than the indulgence of my fondest hopes. Thus stimulated by encouragement, and animated by success, I undertook other operations of a similar tendency, which with gratitude I acknowledge were subsequently crowned with similar rewards. After such gratifying satisfaction, it would be silly affectation not to declare, though no words can express, my sense of public approbation; and implicitly to confess my feelings, that I may not be mistaken, and so become open either to praise or censure which I do not merit. Many have imagined, and some few have

VOL. I.

publicly asserted, that having, with scanty literary education, been
brought up an engraver, the whole of my department has been
confined to the figures and embellishments; and that I have
had very little, or indeed no share in the composition of the history or observations. But my education was not so scanty as
many imagine; I was sent early to a good school, and regularly
kept there; and from the freshest vernal years of my infancy, was
enraptured with nature, and as Nature's Great Poet observes,

" In this my life, exempt from public haunt,
" Found tongues in trees, books by the running brooks,
" Sermons in stones, and good in every thing."

I feel it therefore a duty to myself, as well as to the public, to
aver, that I have already acknowledged what share others have
had in this department in the earlier portions of my works,
which has subsequently been so ameliorated and increased, that
I may justly call it my own; and such communications as I have
since received from friends and kind-hearted intelligent strangers, generally dispersed in their respective places (being too
numerous to particularize) it will both now and hereafter be my
highest pleasure thankfully to acknowledge, by a respectful
mention of their names.

First, to G. T. Fox, Esq. of Westoe, for his indefatigable exertions in searching the repositories of the metropolis, for, and
procuring the loan of, many rare birds, that enrich this, and
were not in former editions.

To John E. Bowman, Esq. Banker, Wrexham, for some ingenious investigations into the physical organization of the interior parts of birds; shewing the wonderful adaptations of a be-
nevolent Providence.

For a perspicuous and discriminative elucidation of the difficult, and hitherto disentangled, tribe of the Willow Wrens, as
well as for specimens carefully and kindly sent from Shropshire,
I am indebted to John Clavering Wood, Esq. of Marsh Hall,
Salop.

And last, though far from least, to his friend and mine,* John

---

* My kind friend, Counsellor Dovaston, fervent and fond in his admiration of Nature, uses in his minute observations on birds, a small spy-
glass which he can instantly and silently draw out to three distinct foci,
and which he facetiously calls his *Ornithoscope.* By this he has acquired
numerous points hitherto unknown. The following extract from one of
the many animated letters of this gentlemen to me, is highly interesting;
and may induce some readers to put his plan into practice. " My friends
imagine these groves are visited by more species of birds than other
places; and kindly tell me the pretty warblers know I am fond of them :
but this arises from my devoting more attention to, and pointing out
their varieties and habits. Every place abounds with delights to those
who have eyes and hearts alive to Nature. The *foraminous* birds I ac-
commodate with artificial building-places in the woods; and others after
their kind. I have also a contrivance for feeding and alluring even the
shyer birds close to my residence, particularly in the Winter months,

F. M. Dovaston, Esq. A. M. of Westfelton, near Shrewsbury, for a great variety of spirited remarks on numerous birds, silently incorporated through the body of the work; as well as for the warm and extensive interest his valued friendship has shewn to it, and to all my concerns.

By such assistance, and my own incessant labours, I have as concisely as consistent with each subject, given every important fact, and discriminative characteristic, which I either knew from fond observation, discovered by intense research, or procured from the more favourable opportunities of others. But industry however unwearied, has often to work in the dark, and enthusiasm however honest, is often dazzled with too much light: each enfeebled by a transition from one to the other; so must many an object be either distorted from imperfect inspection, or omitted from total obscurity.

I have had no respect to opinions, begotten by superstition, or fostered by credulity; yet herein it has never been my intention wantonly to wound the feeble, or insult the really pious. It has been an undeviating principle with me that TRUTH is to bend to nothing, but all to her: and I devoutly thank the Author of Truth for giving me an independent spirit to revere and promote what I believe to be His laws, unseduced by the allurements of interest, and unawed by the clamours of the multitude. I have studied to give perspicuity to facts, facility to fancy, and permanency to instruction.

The conscious integrity of my intention imparts a reasonable expectancy of a continuation of the happiness I have hitherto enjoyed in this life, and a cheerful hope of the eternal existence hereafter; and with these feelings, I offer kindly and respectfully, to liberal and enlightened minds, the last edition of this work, which I may, probably, at my advanced age, live to

that affords me lively amusement. From a tree up to the wall, near my book-room window, a strong, but fine, cord is stretched to another tree at a small distance, crossing the window obliquely : along this runs an iron hook or ring, to which is appended by three harpsichord wires, in the manner of a scale, a trencher with a rim, and perforated slightly to let out the rain. It is suspended beyond the reach of dogs and cats, by whom it was frequently robbed when I had it on a post. This I trim with food, and with a wand from within, can slide it to and fro along the line. It also acts as a coarse hygrometer (particularly if the cord be well twisted, and occasionally saturated with salt) rising previous to rain, and falling before dry weather. I have also perches about and near it, and fasten half-picked bones and flaps of mutton to the trees. During one snowy day I enumerated, with our learned friend Mr Wood, no less than twenty-three sorts of birds, on and about my *Ornithotrophe*, as I humourously denominate it. The Nuthatch is one of the most amusing of my airy, or fairy, guests, by his fanciful and rapid attitudes, hanging under the trencher, and pertinaciously jobbing and stocking at the bones, or hammering the nuts I fasten in the chinks of trees. The proud and busy World may sneer at my simple and inoffensive amusements; but my heart and mind owe to the contemplation of Nature many an hour of sterling happiness, which I would not exchange for all the glare and tinsel of what is, most properly, called fashionable life.

" Ducite ab urbe domum, mea carmina, ducite Daphnim."

republish; though if it please Heaven to allow me the blessings of health and sight, I shall continue to throw off my inoffensive fancies, wherein I perceive no deficiency of imagination; and apply my graphic labours, whereof I seldom feel wearied: it being my firm resolution not to claim the privileges of senility, or suffer inert idleness to encroach on reasonable repose.

Thomas Bewick

NEWCASTLE UPON TYNE, JULY, 1826.

" O Nature ! how in every charm supreme ;
   Thy votaries feast on raptures ever new !
O for the voice and fire of seraphim
   To sing thy glories with devotion due !
Blest be the day I 'scap'd the wrangling crew,
   From Pyrrho's maze, and Epicurus' sty ;
And held high converse with the godlike few,
   Who to th' enraptur'd heart, and ear, and eye,
Teach beauty, virtue, truth, and love, and melody !
   * * * * * * * * * * * * * *
One part, one little part, we dimly scan
Thro' the dark medium of Life's fev'rish dream,
   Yet dare arraign the whole stupendous plan,
If but that little part incongruous seem,
   Nor is that part, perhaps, what mortals deem :
Oft from apparent ill our blessings rise.
   O then renounce that impious self-esteem
That aims to trace the secrets of the skies,
   For thou art but of dust :—be humble, and be wise."

THE ORIGINAL PREFACE.

To those who attentively consider the subject of Natural History, as displayed in the animal creation, it will appear, that though much has been done to explore the intricate paths of Nature, and follow her through all her various windings, much yet remains to be done before the great œconomy is completely developed. Notwithstanding the laborious and not unsuccessful inquiries of ingenious men in all ages, the subject is far from being exhausted. Systems have been formed and exploded, and new ones have appeared in their stead; but, like skeletons injudiciously put together, they give but an imperfect idea of that order and symmetry to which they are intended to be subservient: they have, however, their use, but it is chiefly the skilful practitioner who is enabled to profit by them; to the less informed they appear obscure and perplexing, and too frequently deter him from the great object of his pursuit.

To investigate, with any tolerable degree of success, the more retired and distant parts of the animal œconomy, is a task of no small difficulty. An enquiry so desirable and so eminently useful would require the united efforts of many to give it the desired success. Men of leisure, of all descriptions, residing in the country, could scarcely find a more delightful employment than in attempting to elucidate, from their own observations, the various branches of Natural

History, and in communicating them to others.   Something
like a society in each county, for the purpose of collecting
a variety of these observations, as well as for general correspondence, would be extremely useful.   Much might be expected from a combination of this kind, extending through
every part of the kingdom ; a general mode of communication might be thereby established, in order to ascertain the
changes which are continually taking place, particularly
among the feathered tribes ; the times of their appearing
and disappearing would be carefully noted ; the differences
of age, sex, food, &c. would claim a particular degree of attention, and would be the means of correcting the errors
which have crept into the works of some of the most emi-
nent ornithologists, from an over-anxious desire of increasing
the number of species : but it is reserved, perhaps, for times
of greater tranquillity, when mankind become more enlightened, and see clearly the vast importance of a knowledge of every department of Natural History ; or when
the mind becomes less engaged in the vicious, unprofitable,
or frivolous pursuits of the world, and in lieu of such,
leisure shall be found fully to devote its attention to those
objects which enlarge its powers, give dignity to its exertions, and carry into the fullest effect, plans for investigations of this sort,—that mistakes will be rectified respecting
birds, and their beauties and uses appreciated, and that
they will attract their due share of attention.

As a naturalist no author has been more successful than
the celebrated Count de Buffon : despising the restraints
which methodical arrangements generally impose, he ranges
at large through the various walks of Nature, and describes
her with a brilliancy of colouring which only the most lively
imagination could suggest.   It must, however, be allowed,
that in many instances this ingenious philosopher has over-
stepped the bounds of Nature, and, in giving the reins to his

own luxuriant fancy, has been too frequently hurried into the wild paths of conjecture and romance. The late Mr White, of Selborne, has added much to the general stock of knowledge on this delightful subject, by attentively and faithfully recording whatever fell under his own observation, and by liberal communications to others.

As far as we could, consistently with the plan laid down in the following work, we have consulted, and we trust with some advantage, the works of Willoughby, Ray, and other naturalists. In the arrangement of the various classes, as well as in the descriptive part, we have taken as guides, our intelligent and indefatigable countrymen, Pennant and Latham,* to whose elegant and useful labours the world is indebted for a fund of the most rational entertainment, and who will be remembered by every lover of Nature as long as her works have power to charm. The communications with which we have been favoured by those gentlemen who were so good as to notice our growing work, have been generally acknowledged, each in its proper place; it remains only that we be permitted to insert this testimony of our grateful sense of them.

In a few instances we have ventured to depart from the usual method of classification: by placing the hard billed birds, or those which live chiefly on seeds, next to those of the Pie kind, there seems to be a more regular gradation downwards, since only a few anomalous birds, such as the Cuckoo, Hoopoe, Nuthatch, &c. intervene. The soft-billed birds, or those which subsist chiefly on worms, insects, and such like, are by this mode placed altogether, beginning with those of the Lark kind. To this we must observe, that, by dividing the various families of birds into two grand di-

---

* The works of Col. Montagu have also been consulted in preparing the later editions for the press.

visions, viz. Land and Water, a number of tribes have thereby been included among the latter, which can no otherwise be denominated Water Birds than as they occasionally seek their food in moist places, by small streamlets, or on the seashore ; such as the Curlew, Woodcock, Snipe, Sandpiper, and many others. These, with such as do not commit themselves wholly to the waters, are thrown into a separate division, under the denomination of Waders. To this class we have ventured to remove the Kingfisher, and the Water Ouzel ; the former lives entirely on fish, is constantly found on the margins of still waters, and may with greater propriety be denominated a Water Bird than many which come under that description ; the latter seems to have no connection with those birds among which it is usually classed ; it is generally found among rapid running streams, in which it chiefly delights, and from which it derives its support.

It may be proper to observe, that while one of the editors of this work was engaged in preparing the cuts, which are faithfully drawn from Nature, and engraved upon wood, the compilation of the descriptions of the first Edition *(of the Land Birds)* was undertaken by the other, subject, however, to the corrections of his friend, whose habits had led him to a more intimate acquaintance with this branch of Natural History : the compiler, therefore, is answerable for the defects which may be found in this part of the undertaking, concerning which he has little to say, but that it was the production of those hours which could be spared from a laborious employment, and on that account he hopes the severity of criticism will be spared, and that it will be received with that indulgence which has been already experienced on a former occasion.

Newcastle upon Tyne, September, 1797.

INTRODUCTION

TO THE

HISTORY OF BRITISH LAND BIRDS.

I<small>N</small> no part of the animal creation are the wisdom, the goodness, and the bounty of Providence displayed in a more lively manner than in the structure, formation, and various endowments of the feathered tribes. The symmetry and elegance discoverable in their outward appearance, although highly pleasing to the sight, are yet of much greater importance when considered with respect to their peculiar habits and modes of living, to which they are eminently subservient.

Instead of the large head and formidable jaws, the deep capacious chest, the brawny shoulders, and sinewy legs of the quadrupeds, we observe the pointed beak, the long and pliant neck, the gently swelling shoulder, the expansive wings, the tapering tail, the light and bony feet; which are all wisely calculated to assist and accelerate their motion through the yielding air. Every part of their frame is formed for lightness and buoyancy; their bodies are covered with a soft and delicate plumage, so disposed as to protect them from the intense cold of the atmosphere through which they pass; their wings are made of the lightest materials, and yet the force with which they strike the air is so great as to impel their bodies forward with astonishing rapidity, whilst the tail serves the purpose of a rudder to direct them to the different objects of their pursuit. The internal structure of birds is no less wisely adapted to the same purposes; all the bones are light and thin, and all the muscles, except those which are appropriated to the purpose of moving the wings, are extremely delicate and light; the lungs are placed close to the back-bone and ribs; the air entering into them by a communication from the windpipe, passes through, and is conveyed into a number of membraneous cells which lie upon the sides of the pericardium, and communicate with those of the sternum. In some birds these cells are continued down the wings, and extended even to the pinions, thigh-bones, and other parts of the body, which can be filled and distended with air at the pleasure of the animal.

The extreme singularity of this almost universal diffusion of air through the bodies of birds, has excited a strong desire to discover the intention of Nature in producing a conformation so extraordinary. The ingenious Mr Hunter imagined that it might be intended to assist the animal in the act of flying, by increasing its bulk and strength, without adding to its weight. This opinion was corroborated by considering, that the feathers of birds, and particularly those of the wings, contain a great quantity of air.   In opposition to this, he informs us that the Ostrich, which does not fly, is nevertheless provided with air-cells dispersed through its body; that the Woodcock, and some other flying birds, are not so liberally supplied with these cells; yet, he elsewhere observes, that it may be laid down as a general rule, that in birds who are enabled to take the highest and longest flights, as the Eagle, this extension or diffusion of air is carried further than in others; and, with regard to the Ostrich, though it is deprived of the power of flying, it runs with amazing rapidity, and consequently requires similar resources of air. It seems therefore to be proved, evidently, that this general diffusion of air through the bodies of birds is of infinite use to them, not only in their long and laborious flights, but likewise in preventing their respiration from being stopped or interrupted by the rapidity of their motion through a resisting medium.   Were it possible for man to move with the swiftness of a Swallow, the actual resistance of the air, as he is not provided with internal reservoirs similar to those of birds, would soon suffocate him.*

Birds may be distinguished, like quadrupeds, into two kinds or classes—granivorous and carnivorous; like quadrupeds too, there are some that hold a middle nature, and partake of both.   Granivorous birds are furnished with larger intestines, and proportionally longer, than those of the carnivorous kind.   Their food, which consists of grain of various sorts, is conveyed whole and entire into the first stomach or craw, where it undergoes a partial dilution by a liquor

* May not this universal diffusion of air through the bodies of birds, account for the superior heat of this class of animals? The separation of oxygen from respirable air, and its mixture with the blood by means of the lungs, is supposed, by the ingenious Dr Crawford, to be the efficient cause of animal heat.

secreted from the glands and spread over its surface; it is then received into another species of stomach, where it is further diluted; after which it is transmitted into the gizzard, or true stomach, consisting of two very strong muscles, covered externally with a tendinous substance, and lined with a thick membrane of prodigious power and strength : in this place the food is completely triturated, and rendered fit for the operation of the gastric juices. The extraordinary powers of the gizzard in comminuting the food, so as to prepare it for digestion, would exceed all credibility, were they not supported by incontrovertible facts founded upon experiments. In order to ascertain the strength of these stomachs, the ingenious Spalanzani made the following curious and very interesting experiments :—Tin tubes, full of grain, were forced into the stomachs of Turkies, and after remaining twenty hours, were found to be broken, compressed, and distorted in the most irregular manner.* In proceeding further the same author relates, that the stomach of a Cock, in the space of twenty-four hours, broke off the angles of a piece of rough jagged glass, and upon examining the gizzard no wound or laceration appeared. Twelve strong needles were firmly fixed in a ball of lead, the points of which projected about a quarter of an inch from the surface; thus armed, it was covered with a case of paper, and forced down the throat of a Turkey; the bird retained it a day and a half, without shewing the least symptom of uneasiness; the points of all the needles were broken off close to the surface of the ball, except two or three, of which the stumps projected a little. The same author relates another experiment, seemingly still more cruel : he fixed twelve small lancets, very sharp, in a similar ball of lead, which was given in the same manner to a Turkey-cock,

* Spalanzani's Dissertations, vol. 1, page 12.

and left eight hours in the stomach; at the expiration of
which the organ was opened, but nothing appeared except
the naked ball, the twelve lancets having been broken to
pieces, the stomach remaining perfectly sound and entire.
From these curious and well-attested facts, we may conclude,
that the stones so often found in the stomachs of many of
the feathered tribes, are highly useful in comminuting grain
and other hard substances which constitute their food.
" The stones," says the celebrated Mr Hunter, " assist in
grinding down the grain, and, by separating its parts, allow
the gastric juices to come more readily into contact with
it." Thus far the conclusion coincides with the experiments which have just been related. We may observe still
further, that stones thus taken into the stomachs of birds,
are seldom known to pass with the fæces, but being ground
down and separated by the powerful action of the gizzard,
are mixed with the food, and, no doubt, contribute essentially to the health of the animal.

Granivorous birds partake much of the nature and disposition of herbivorous quadrupeds. In both, the number of
their stomachs, the length and capacity of their intestines,
and the quality of their food, are very similar; they are likewise both distinguished by the gentleness of their tempers
and manners. Contented with the seeds of plants, with
fruits, insects, and worms, their chief attention is directed
to procuring food, hatching and rearing their offspring, and
avoiding the snares of men, and the attacks of birds of prey,
and other rapacious animals. They are a mild and gentle
race, and are in general so tractable as easily to be domesticated. Man, attentive and watchful to every thing condu-
cive to his interest, has not failed to avail himself of these
dispositions, and has judiciously selected from the numbers
which every way surround him, those which are most prolific, and consequently most profitable: of these the Hen,

the Goose, the Turkey, and the Duck are the most considerable, and form an inexhaustible store of rich, wholesome, and nutritious food.

Carnivorous birds are distinguished by those endowments and powers with which they are furnished by Nature for the purpose of procuring their food : they are provided with wings of great length, the muscles which move them being proportionally large and strong, whereby they are enabled to keep long upon the wing in search of their prey ; they are armed with strong hooked bills, and sharp and formidable claws ; they have also large heads, short necks, strong and brawny thighs, and a sight so acute and piercing, as to enable them to view their prey from the greatest heights in the air, upon which they dart with inconceivable swiftness and undeviating aim ; their stomachs are smaller than those of the granivorous kinds, and their intestines are much shorter. The analogy between the structure of rapacious birds and carnivorous quadrupeds is obvious; both of them are provided with weapons which indicate destruction and rapine ; their manners are fierce and unsocial; and they seldom live together in flocks, like the inoffensive granivorous tribes. When not on the wing, rapacious birds retire to the tops of sequestered rocks, or to the depths of extensive forests, where they conceal themselves in sullen and gloomy solitude. Those which feed on carrion are endowed with a sense of smelling so exquisite, as to enable them to scent putrid carcases at astonishing distances.

Without the means of conveying themselves with great swiftness from one place to another, birds could not easily subsist : the food which Nature has so bountifully provided for them is so irregularly distributed, that they are obliged to take long journies to distant parts in order to gain the necessary supplies : at one time it is given in great abundance ; at another it is administered with a very sparing hand ; and

this is one cause of those migrations so peculiar to the feathered tribes.   Besides the want of food, there are two
other causes of migration, viz. the want of a proper temperature of air, and a convenient situation for the great work
of breeding and rearing their young.   Such birds as migrate
to great distances are alone denominated *birds of passage;*
but most birds are, in some measure, birds of passage, although they do not migrate to places remote from their former habitations.   At particular times of the year most birds
remove from one country to another, or from the more inland districts towards the shores : the times of these migrations or flittings are observed with most astonishing order
and punctuality; but the secrecy of their departure, and
the suddenness of their re-appearance, have involved the
subject of migration in general in great difficulty.   Much of
this difficulty arises from our not being able to account for
their means of subsistence during the long flights of many of
those birds which are obliged to cross immense tracts of water before they arrive at the places of their destination : accustomed to measure distance by the speed of those animals
with which we are well acquainted, we are apt to overlook
the superior velocity with which birds are carried forward in
the air, and the ease with which they continue their exertions, for a much longer time than can be done by the
strongest quadruped.

Our swiftest horses are supposed to go at the rate of a
mile in somewhat less than two minutes ; and we have one
instance on record of a horse being tried, which went at the
rate of nearly a mile in one minute, but that was only for
the small space of a second of time.*   In this and similar instances we find, that an uncommon degree of exertion is attended with its usual consequences, debility, and a total

* See History of Quadrupeds.

want of power to continue that exertion; but the case is very different with birds; their motions are not impeded by similar causes; they glide through the air with a quickness superior to that of the swiftest quadruped, and they can continue on the wing with equal speed for a considerable length of time. Now, if we can suppose a bird to go at the rate of only half a mile in a minute, for the space of twenty-four hours, it will have gone over, in that time, an extent of more than seven hundred miles, which is sufficient to account for almost the longest migration; but if aided by a favourable current of air, there is reason to suppose that the same journey may be performed in a much shorter space of time. To these observations we may add, that the sight of birds is peculiarly quick and piercing; and from the advantage they possess in being raised to considerable heights in the air, they are enabled, with a sagacity peculiar to instinctive knowledge, to discover the route they are to take, from the appearance of the atmosphere, the clouds, the direction of the winds, and other causes; so that, without having recourse to improbable modes, it is easy to conceive, from the velocity of their speed alone, that most birds may transport themselves to countries lying at great distances, and across vast tracts of ocean.

The following observations from Catesby are very applicable, and shall conclude our remarks on this head:—" The manner of their journeyings may vary according as the structure of their bodies enables them to support themselves in the air. Birds with short wings, such as the Redstart, Blackcap, &c. may pass by gradual and slower movements; and there seems no necessity for a precipitate passage, as every day affords an increase of warmth, and a continuance of food. It is probable these itinerants may perform their journey in the night time, in order to avoid ravenous birds, and other dangers which day-light may expose them to. The flight of the smaller birds of passage across the seas has, by many, been considered as wonderful, and especially with regard to those with short wings, among which Quails seem, by their structure, little adapted for long flights; nor are they ever seen to continue on the wing for any length of time, and yet their ability for such flights cannot be doubted. The coming of these birds is certain and regular, from every year's experience, but the cause and manner of their departure have not always been so happily accounted for; in short, all we know of the matter ends in this observation,—that Providence has created a great variety of birds and other animals with constitutions and inclinations adapted to their several wants and necessities, as well as to the different degrees of heat and cold in the several climates of the world, whereby no country is destitute of inhabitants, and has given them appetites for the productions of those countries whose temperature is suited to their nature, as well as knowledge and ability to seek and find them out."

The migration of the Swallow tribe has been noticed by almost every writer on the natural history of birds, and various opinions have been formed respecting their disappearance, and the state in which they exist during that interval. Some naturalists suppose that they do not leave this island at the end of autumn, but that they lie in a torpid state, till the beginning of summer, in the banks of rivers, in the hollows of decayed trees, in holes and crevices of old buildings, in sand banks and the like.   That those which have been left behind, as well as other birds of passage, as soon as the cold weather sets in, fall into a torpid state, and remain so till the return of warmth brings them out of it, are facts which are now not doubted.   But as to their passing the winter immersed in water, and being found there in "clusters, mouth to mouth, wing to wing, foot to foot," and of their creeping down reeds to their subaqueous retreats, as

believed by Klein, as well as the similar description trans-
lated from Kalm's travels in North America, though these
marvellous narratives have been *credited* by some ornithologists, yet nothing can exceed the absurdity of both accounts.*

---

* Extract of a letter from the Rev. Wm Floyer Cornish, of Totness,
Devon, dated April 10, 1826 :—" Being much interested in these delightful
little visitors, (the Summer migratory birds) and at the same time very
desirous to try whether I could keep them in health during the winter,
I will inform you of the result of my experiments.

" I began with Nightingales, which I procured from London, and have
kept them in perfect health, and stout in song, for several years ; those
that I have had have been old birds, taken in the spring soon after their
arrival in England ; they seldom recommenced their song till towards
the end of the year, when they sang as finely as those in their native
woods. Having succeeded so well with " the leaders of the vernal
chorus," my next attempt was with the Black-caps, but these have been
nestlings. I have had two for the last three years, in perfect health and
full song ; another, which I reared last year, is at this moment roaring
away most powerfully. I have kept also the larger as well as the smaller
White-throats ; three of the latter description, reared from the nest,
have been with me for more than three years ; one of them while I am
now writing is warbling his little song very sweetly ; two of them are
cocks and the other a hen, and they live very happily together, and are
perfectly tame ; they are so gentle and familiar, that they will take any
little delicacy from our fingers or our lips, and are particularly fond of
sugar and fruit, both of which I have seldom omitted giving to them, as
well as to the Black-caps, every day ; and at this season of the year they
regularly seem to expect their bit of apple. The song of the larger White-
throat is much louder and more agreeable, but I have none of them at
present. In consequence of seeing in your history of the Swallow, the
successful result of a gentleman in London to preserve them during the
winter, I resolved to make the attempt of rearing some nestlings, which
I did last year. On the 12th of July, a nest was brought to me by my desire, containing three young ones pretty well fledged ; one of them, which
I think was a hen, a few weeks after I had it, forced its way through the
wires of the cage, and flew away perfectly strong, and joined others of its
species which were flying near the house : the others, which are cock
birds, have remained quite healthy during the winter, and cheered us
particularly with their simple song on Christmas-day. They moulted

The celebrated Mr John Hunter informs us, " that he had dissected many Swallows, but found nothing in them different from other birds as to the organs of respiration," and therefore concludes that it is highly absurd to suppose, that terrestrial animals can remain any long time under water without being drowned.

We have observed a single Swallow so late as the latter end of October; others assert that they have often been seen till near Christmas. Mr White, in his Natural History of Selborne, mentions having seen a House Martin flying about in November, long after the general migration had taken place. Many more instances might be given of such late appearances.

To the many on record we shall add the following, which we received from a very intelligent master of a vessel, who, whilst he was sailing early in the spring between the islands of Minorca and Majorca, saw great numbers of Swallows flying northward, many of which, from fatigue, alighted on the rigging of the ship in the evening, but disappeared before morning. After all our inquiries into this branch of natural œconomy, much yet remains to be known, and we may conclude in the words of the pleasing and accurate Mr White, " that whilst we observe with delight, with how much ardour and punctuality these little birds obey the

towards the latter end of the year, but during the whole of this weakening period they did not cease to sing, not only during the day, but in the evening; in the cold weather the cage was well wrapped up and covered over with green baize : as the weather is now become milder, their covering is partially withdrawn: they have always been kept in a warm room, and occasionally been placed near a window; but when it was at all cold, they retired to their perch, which is covered with baize, as far as possible from it. Their food is the same which I give to the other summer birds— beef, mutton, veal, or lamb, not over dressed, chopped very small, and mixed with hard eggs, yellow as well as white, and a little chopped hempseed, on which they have thriven very well."

strong impulse towards migration or hiding, imprinted on
their minds by their great Creator, it is with no small degree of mortification we reflect, that after all our pains and
inquiries, we are not yet quite certain to what regions they
do migrate, and are still farther embarrassed to find that
some actually do not migrate at all."

> " Amusive birds ! say where your hid retreat,
> " When the frost rages, and the tempests beat;
> " Whence your return, by such nice instinct led,
> " When Spring, sweet season, lifts her bloomy head !
> " Such baffled searches mock man's prying pride,
> " The GOD of NATURE is your secret guide !"

Most birds, at certain seasons, live together in pairs ; the
union is formed in the spring, and generally continues whilst
the united efforts of both are necessary in forming their
temporary habitations, and in rearing and maintaining their
offspring.   Eagles and other birds of prey continue their attachment for a much longer time, and sometimes for life.
The nests of birds are constructed with such exquisite art, as
to exceed the utmost exertion of human ingenuity to imitate
them.   Their mode of building, the materials they make use
of, as well as the situations they select, are as various as the
different kinds of birds, and are all admirably adapted to their
several wants and necessities.   Birds of the same species,
whatever region of the globe they inhabit, collect the same
materials, arrange them in the same manner, and make
choice of similar situations for fixing the places of their temporary abodes.   To describe minutely the different kinds of
nests, the various substances of which they are composed,
and the judicious choice of situations, would swell this part
of our work much beyond its due bounds. Every part of the
world furnishes materials for the aerial architects : leaves and
small twigs, roots and dried grass, mixed with clay, serve for

the external ; whilst moss, wool, fine hair, and the softest
animal and vegetable downs, form the warm internal part
of these commodious dwellings.   The following beautiful
lines from Thomson are highly descriptive of the busy scene
which takes place during the time of nidification :—

" . . . . Some to the holly hedge,
" Nestling, repair, and to the thicket some ;
" Some to the rude protection of the thorn
" Commit their feeble offspring : the cleft tree
" Offers its kind concealment to a few,
" Their food its insects, and its moss their nests :
" Others apart, far in the grassy dale
" Or roughening waste their humble texture weave :
" But most in woodland solitudes delight,
" In unfrequented glooms or shaggy banks,
" Steep, and divided by a babbling brook,
" Whose murmurs soothe them all the live-long day,
" When by kind duty fix'd. Among the roots
" Of hazel, pendent o'er the plaintive stream,
" They frame the first foundation of their domes,
" Dry sprigs of trees, in artful fabric laid,
" And bound with clay together. Now 'tis nought
" But restless hurry through the busy air,
" Beat by unnumber'd wings. The Swallow sweeps
" The slimy pool to build the hanging house
" Intent : and often from the careless back
" Of herds and flocks, a thousand tugging bills
" Pluck hair and wool ; and oft, when unobserved,
" Steal from the barn a straw ; till soft and warm,
" Clean and complete, their habitation grows."

After the business of incubation is over, and the young are
sufficiently able to provide for themselves, the nests are always abandoned by the parents, excepting by those of the
Eagle kind.

The various gifts and endowments which the great Author
of Nature has so liberally bestowed upon his creatures, de-

mand, in a peculiar manner, the attention of the curious
Naturalist ;* among the feathered tribes in particular, there

* The following remarks, applicable to this subject, are taken from a
letter written by J. E. Bowman, Esq. on the Anatomy of the Woodpecker.
" Though the tip of the tongue in this genus, is well known to be horny
and barbed, another peculiarity of structure connected with it, and without which it could not perform its office, does not appear to have been
noticed by Naturalists. In the back part of the palate is inserted a longitudinal groove, which tapers to a point outwards, and is fringed with stiff
hairs pointing towards the throat. Without this provision, it would be difficult to conceive how the bird could so easily and speedily detach its food
from the barbs of the tongue, as it is known to do, particularly as the groove
in the palate is placed much too backward, for the tip of the former, in its
natural position, ever to reach it; and even if it could draw it in so far,
the peculiar direction of the hairs, would prevent their action. We
must therefore infer (though the motion is performed with such celerity
that we can never expect to observe it) that the tongue is taken into the
mouth in a reflected position, like that of the Frog, and that the tip of it
is drawn through the groove, the sharp hairs of which scrape off the insects from the barbs, while the deglutition is assisted by the tubercles on
the surface of the tongue during the first part of the operation of drawing
it into the mouth. The glottis is very large, and is singularly placed on
the surface of the tongue, which is perforated by the trachea ; and this
doubtless is the cause of the singularly harsh and inharmonious note by
which this interesting bird is distinguished. I have detailed these particulars, perhaps rather tediously, in the hope of drawing the attention of
the young Naturalist to study any peculiarity he may observe in the organization of the animal kingdom. He may set out with the firm as-
surance, that nothing is made in vain, and that the apparently most insignificant organ has some important function to perform, though we
cannot always discover it; but he must constantly keep in view, that
a cautious and scientific application of the inferences, that will suggest
themselves to him, is the only basis on which a correct and rational study
of the philosophy of Zoology can be built; and this is a field so extensive, and hitherto so little trod, that every careful observer may calcu-
late upon adding something to promote it. To be merely acquainted
with an artificial system, however perfectly, with the names of genera or
species, though it be absolutely necessary, ought not to satisfy him who
professes the study of Nature. The legitimate aim is to lead the mind to
the Great Author, who has so wonderfully suited every creature to its
sphere, and furnished it with capacities for enjoying happiness. Wit-
nessing this, every where profusely displayed, we must be filled at every
step, with a more sublime, rational, and delightful adoration of a Being
so boundlessly powerful."

is much room, in this respect, for minute and attentive investigation. In pursuing our inquiries into that system of œconomy, by which every part of Nature is upheld and preserved, we are struck with wonder in observing the havock and destruction which every where prevail throughout the various orders of beings inhabiting the earth. Our humanity is interested in that law of Nature which devotes to destruction myriads of creatures to support and continue the existence of others; but although it is not allowed us to unravel the mysterious workings of Nature through all her parts, or unfold her deep designs, we are, nevertheless, strongly led to the consideration of the means by which individuals, as well as species, are preserved. The weak are frequently enabled to elude the pursuits of the strong by flight or stratagem; some are screened from the pursuits of their enemies by an arrangement of colours happily assimilated to the places which they most frequent, and where they find either food or repose: thus the Wryneck is scarcely to be distinguished from the bark of the tree on which it feeds; or the Snipe from the soft and mossy ground by the springs of water which it frequents: the Great Plover finds its chief security in stony places, to which its colours are so nicely adapted, that the most exact observer may be very easily deceived. The attentive ornithologist will not fail to discover numerous instances of this kind, such as the Partridge, Plover, Quail, &c.

Some are indebted to the brilliancy of their colours as the means of alluring their prey; of this the Kingfisher is a remarkable instance, and deserves to be particularly noticed. This beautiful bird has been observed, in some sequestered place near the edge of a rivulet, exposing the vivid colours of its breast to the full rays of the sun, and fluttering with expanded wings over the smooth surface of the water; the fish, attracted by the brightness and splendour of the appearance, are detained whilst the wily bird darts down upon them, with unerring aim. We do not say that the mode of taking fish by torch light has been derived from this practised by the Kingfisher, but every one must be struck by the similarity of the means. Others, again, derive the same advantage from the simplicity of their exterior appearance; of this the Heron will serve for an example. He may frequently be seen standing motionless by the edge of a piece of water, waiting patiently the approach of his prey, which he never fails to seize as soon as it comes within reach of his long neck; he then re-assumes his former position, and continues to wait with the same patient attention as before.

Most of the smaller birds are supported, especially when young, by a profusion of caterpillars, small worms, and insects; on these they feed, and thus they contribute to preserve the vegetable world from destruction. This is contrary to the commonly received opinion, that birds, particularly Sparrows, do much mischief in destroying the labours of the gardener and the husbandman. It has been observed, " that a single pair of Sparrows, during the time they are feeding their young, will destroy about four thousand caterpillars weekly; they likewise feed their young with butterflies and other winged insects, each of which, if not destroyed in this manner, would be productive of many thousands of caterpillars."- Swallows are almost continually upon the wing, and in their curious winding flights destroy immense quantities of flies and other insects, which are continually floating in the air, and which, if not destroyed by these birds, would render it unfit for the purposes of life and health.

That active little bird the Tomtit, which is generally supposed hostile to the young and tender buds that appear in the spring, when attentively observed, may be seen running up and down among the branches, and picking up the eggs*

* On these they almost solely live in winter.

of insects, maggots, &c. or the small worms that are concealed in the blossoms, and which would effectually destroy
the fruit. As the season advances, various other small
birds, such as the Red-breast, Wren, Hedge-Warbler,
White-throat, Redstart, &c. are all engaged in the same
useful work, and may be observed examining every leaf, and
feeding upon the insects which they find beneath them.
These are a few instances of that superintending providential
care, which is continually exerted in preserving the various
ranks and orders of beings in the scale of animated Nature;
and although it is permitted that myriads of individuals
should every moment be destroyed, not a single species is
lost, but every link of the great chain remains unbroken.

Great Britain produces a more abundant variety of birds
than most northern countries, owing to the various condition
of our lands, from the highest state of cultivation to that of
the wildest, most mountainous, and woody. The great
quantities of berries and other kinds of fruit produced in our
hedges, heaths, and plantations, bring small birds in great
numbers, and birds of prey in consequence : our shores, and
the numerous little islands adjacent to them, afford shelter
and protection to an infinite variety of almost all kinds of
water fowl. To enumerate the various kinds of birds that
visit this island annually will not, we presume, be unaccept-
able to our readers, nor improper in this part of our work.
The following are selected chiefly from Mr White's Natural
History of Selborne, and are arranged nearly in the order of
their appearing :—

1 Wryneck, ... Middle of March
2 Smallest Willow Wren, ... Latter end of ditto
3 House Swallow, ... Middle of April
4 Martin, ... Ditto
5 Sand Martin, ... Ditto

6	Blackcap, ...	Middle of April
7	Nightingale, ...	Beginning of April
8	Cuckoo, ...	Middle of ditto
9	Middle Willow Wren, ...	Ditto
10	Whitethroat, ...	Ditto
11	Redstart, ...	Ditto
12	Great Plover or Stone Curlew,	End of March
13	Grasshopper Lark, ...	Middle of April
14	Swift, ...	Latter end of ditto
15	Lesser Reed Sparrow, ...	
16	Corn Crake or Land Rail, ...	
17	Largest Willow Wren, ...	End of April
18	Fern Owl, ...	Latter end of May
19	Flycatcher, ...	Middle of ditto.*

To this list of migratory birds, some ornithologists have added the Larks, Ouzels, Thrushes, and Starlings.

Most of the soft-billed birds feed on insects and not on grain or seeds, and therefore usually retire before winter; but the following, though they eat insects, remain with us during the whole year, viz. The Redbreast, Hedge-Warbler, and Wren, which frequent out-houses and gardens, and eat spiders, small worms, crumbs, &c. the Pied, the Yellow, and the Grey Wagtail, which frequent the heads of springs, where the waters seldom freeze, and feed on the aureliæ of insects usually deposited there. Beside these, the Winchat, the Stonechat, and the Golden-crested Wren,† are seen with

* This, according to Mr White, is the latest summer bird of passage; but the arrival of some of the summer birds is very uncertain: those which are the first in some seasons, are the last in others: this can only be determined by their song.

† A pair of these little birds alighted on the deck of a ship, belonging to Newcastle, commanded by John Tone, when the vessel had passed about mid-seas over between Newfoundland and the British shores. The captain nursed them in the cabin with all possible tenderness, but with-

us during the winter ; the latter, though the least of all the British birds, is very hardy, and can endure the utmost severity of our winters. The Wheatear, though not common, sometimes stays the winter with us.—Of the winter birds of passage, the following are the principal, viz.

1. The Redwing.

2. The Fieldfare.—[Both these arrive in great numbers about Michaelmas, and depart about the end of February, or beginning of March, but are sometimes detained by easterly winds till the middle of April.]

3. The Hooded Crow visits us in the beginning of winter, and departs with the Woodcock.

4. The Woodcock appears about Michaelmas, and leaves us about the beginning of March, but is sometimes detained till the middle of April.

5. Snipes are considered by Mr White as birds of passage, though he acknowledges that they frequently breed with us. Mr Pennant remarks, that their young are so frequently found in Britain, that it may be doubted whether they ever entirely leave this island.

6. The Judcock.

7. The Wild Pigeon,—[Of the precise time of its arrival we are not quite certain, but suppose it may be some time in April. Some ornithologists assert that they do not migrate.]

8. The Wild Swan frequents the coasts of this island in large flocks, but is not supposed to breed with us. It has

out success, for they were found the next morning, each with their heads under the other's wing, quite dead ; they most likely had been blown out of their course by a tempest, in their long migratory flight from Sweden, Norway, or Lapland, to their halting places, the Zetland or the Orkney Isles, or had been driven in their last passage to this country, off the land, by adverse gales ; like many thousands of other land birds thus blown to sea to become food for fishes.

been chiefly met with in the northern parts, and is said to arrive at Lingey, one of the Hebrides, in October, and to remain there till March, when it retires more northward to breed.

9. The Wild Goose passes southward in October, and returns northward in April.*

With regard to the Duck kind in general, they are mostly birds of passage. Mr Pennant says, " Of the numerous species that form this genus, we know of no more than five that breed here, viz. the Tame Swan, the Tame Goose, the Shield Duck, the Eider Duck, and a very small number of the Wild Ducks : the rest contribute to form that amazing multitude of water fowls that annually repair from most parts of Europe to the woods and lakes of Lapland and other arctic regions, there to perform the functions of incubation and nutrition in full security. They and their young quit their retreats in September, and disperse themselves over Europe. With us they make their appearance in the beginning of October, circulate first round our shores, and when compelled by severe frost, betake themselves to our lakes and rivers." In winter the Bernacles and Brent Geese appear in vast flocks on the north-west coast of Britain, and leave us in February, when they migrate as far as Lapland, Greenland, or Spitzbergen.

The Solan Geese or Gannets are birds of passage; their first appearance is in March, and they continue till August or September. The long-legged Plover and Sanderling visit

---

* Sometimes, for reasons not yet accounted for by naturalists, they return northward at the latter end of the year.

A flock passed over Newcastle northward on the 6th of December, 1813. Another passed on the 22d of December, 1813.

Another on the 25th of November, 1814.

One passed *southward* on the 12th December, 1814, and they have often since been noticed to pass in the same way.

us in winter only; and it is worthy of remark, that every
species of the Curlews, Woodcocks, Sandpipers, and Plovers, which forsake us in the spring, retire to Sweden, Po-
land, Russia, Norway, and Lapland, to breed, and return
to us as soon as the young are able to fly; for the frosts,
which set in early in those countries, deprive them totally
of the means of subsistence.

Besides these, there is a great variety of birds which perform partial migrations, or flittings, from one part of the
country to another.   During hard winters, when the surface
of the earth is covered with snow, many birds, such as
Larks, Snipes, &c. withdraw from the inland parts of the
country towards the sea shores, in quest of food; others, as
the Wren, the Redbreast, and a variety of small birds, quit
the fields, and approach the habitations of men.   The Chatterer, the Grosbeak, and the Crossbill, are only occasional
visitors, and observe no regular times in making their appearance.   Great numbers of the Chatterer were taken in
the county of Northumberland in the latter end of the years
1789 and 1790, before which they had seldom been observed so far south as that county, but since that time, however,
several have visited the north of England.

The term of life varies greatly in birds, and does not seem
to bear the same proportion to the time of acquiring their
growth, as has been remarked with regard to quadrupeds.
Most birds acquire their full dimensions in a few months,
and are capable of propagation the first summer after they
are hatched.   In proportion to the size of their bodies, birds
possess more vitality, and live longer, than either man or
quadrupeds: notwithstanding the difficulties which arise in
ascertaining the ages of birds, there are instances of great
longevity in many of them.   Geese and Swans have been
known to attain to the age of seventy and upwards; Ravens
are very long-lived birds, they are said sometimes to exceed

a century; Eagles are supposed to arrive at a great age; Pigeons are known to live more than twenty years; and even Linnets and other small birds have been kept in cages from fifteen to twenty years.

To the practical ornithologist there arises a considerable gratification in being able to ascertain the distinguishing characters of birds as they appear at a distance, whether at rest, or during their flight; for not only every genus has something peculiar to itself, but each species has its own appropriate marks, by which a judicious observer may discriminate almost with certainty. Of these, the various modes of flight (whether seen by day light, or heard in their passing at night) afford the most certain and obvious means of distinction, and should be noted with the most careful attention. From the bold and lofty flight of the Eagle, to the short and sudden flittings of the Sparrow or the Wren, there is an ample field for the curious investigator of nature, on which he may dwell with inexpressible delight, tracing the various movements of the feathered nations which every where present themselves to his view. The notes, or, as it may with more propriety be called, the language, of birds, whereby they are enabled to express, in no inconsiderable degree, their various passions, wants, and feelings, must be particularly noticed. By the great power of their voice,* they can communicate their sentiments and intentions to each other, and are enabled to act by mutual concert: that of the wing, by which they can remove from place to place with inconceivable celerity and dispatch, is peculiar to the feathered tribes; it gives them a decided superiority over every species of quadrupeds, and affords them the greatest means of security from those attacks to which their weakness would otherwise expose them. The social instinct a-

* White's Selborne.

mong birds is peculiarly lively and interesting, and likewise proves an effectual means of preservation from the various arts which are made use of to circumvent and destroy them. Individuals may perish, and the species may suffer a diminution of its numbers; but its instincts, habits, and œconomy remain entire.

EXPLANATION

OF THE

TECHNICAL TERMS USED IN THIS WORK:

TO WHICH ARE SUBJOINED

SOME OF THOSE USED BY LINNÆUS AND OTHER ORNITHOLO-
GISTS, DESCRIPTIVE OF THE PARTICULAR PARTS
PECULIAR TO SOME SPECIES.

A—AURICULARS,—feathers which cover the ears.

BB—The BASTARD WING, [*alula spuria*, Linn.] three or five quill-like feathers, placed at a small joint rising at the middle part of the wing.

CC—The LESSER COVERTS of the WINGS, [*tectrices primæ*, Linn.] small feathers that lie in several rows on the bones of the wings. The UNDER COVERTS are those that line the inside of the wings.

DD—The GREATER COVERTS, [*tectrices secundæ*, Linn.] the feathers that lie immediately over the quill feathers and the secondaries.

GG—The PRIMARIES, or PRIMARY QUILLS, [*primores*, Linn.] the largest feathers of the wings: they rise from the first bone.

EE—The SECONDARIES, or SECONDARY QUILLS, [*secondariæ*, Linn.] those that rise from the second bone.

HH—The TERTIALS. These also take their rise from the second bone, at the *elbow joint*, forming a continuation of the secondaries, and seem to do the same with the scapulars, which lie over them. These feathers are so long in some of the *Scolopax* and *Tringa* genera, that when the bird is flying they give it the appearance of having four wings.

SS—The SCAPULARS, or SCAPULAR FEATHERS, take their rise from the shoulders, and cover the sides of the back.

P—COVERTS of the TAIL. [*uropygium*, Linn.] These feathers cover it on the upper side, at the base.

V—The VENT FEATHERS, [*crissum*, Linn.] those that lie from the vent, or *anus*, to the tail underneath.

———

IRIS, (plural IRIDES) the part which surrounds the pupil of the eye.

MANDIBLES,—the upper and under parts of the bill.

COMPRESSED,—flatted at the sides vertically.

DEPRESSED,—flatted horizontally.

CUNEATED,—wedge-shaped.

Head of the Merlin Hawk.

1—The CERE, [*cera*, Linn.] the naked skin which covers the base of the bill, as in the Hawk kind.

2—The ORBITS, [*orbita*, Linn.] the skin which surrounds the eye. It is generally bare, but particularly in the Parrot and the Heron.

Head of the Great Ash-coloured Shrike.

1—When the bill is notched near the tip, as in Shrikes, Thrushes, &c. it is called by Linnæus *rostrum emarginatum.*

2—*Vibrissæ,* (Linn.) are hairs that stand forward like feelers : in some birds they are slender, as in Flycatchers, &c. and point both upwards and downwards, from both the upper and under sides of the mouth.

3—*Capistrum*—a word used by Linnæus to express the short feathers on the forehead, just above the bill. In some birds these feathers fall forward over the nostrils : they quite cover those of the Crow.

Rostrum cultratum, (Linn.) when the edges of the bill are very sharp, as in that of the Crow.

Head of the Night-jar.

1—*Vibrissæ pectinatæ,* (Linn.) These hairs in this bird are very stiff, and spread out on each side like a comb, from the upper sides of the mouth only.

Foot of the Night-jar.

Shewing the middle toe claw SERRATED like a saw. PEC-TINATED signifies toothed like a comb.

Head of the Great-crested Grebe.

2—The LORE, [*Lorum,* Linn.] the space between the bill and the eye, which in this genus is bare, but in other birds is generally covered with feathers.

Foot of the Kingfisher.

Shewing the peculiar structure, in the toes being joined together from their origin to the end joints.

Foot of the Grey Phalarope.

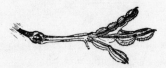

FIN-FOOTED and SCALLOPED, [*pinnatus,* Linn.] as are also those of the Coots.

Foot of the Red-necked Grebe.

Toes furnished on their sides with broad plain membranes. [*Pes lobatus,* Linn.]

Foot of the Cormorant.

Shewing all the four toes connected by webs.

SEMI-PALMATED, [*semi-palmatus*, Linn.] when the middle of the webs reach only about half the length of the toes.

CILIATED, [*lingua ciliata*, Linn.] when the tongue is edged with fine bristles, as in Ducks.

NOSTRILS LINEAR,—when they are extended lengthwise in a line with the bill, as in Divers, &c.

NOSTRILS PERVIOUS,—when they are open, and may be seen through from side to side, as in Gulls, &c.

A Method of dating dead Game. Recommended in Sir Tho-
mas Frankland's " Cautions to Young Sportsmen," ed. 2
page 8.

" The following is a simple method of dating the day on
which birds were killed. Let the six fore toes represent the
six shooting days of the week. The left toe of the left foot
answering for Monday, count from thence to the right toe
of the right foot, which is to pass for Saturday. Let any
portion of that toe which corresponds to the day on which
the bird was killed, be cut off. If a part of one or more
toes has been shot off, cut that which is to register the day
still shorter. I am aware that a whole foot may be carried
away; but in general the practice will answer. Perhaps in
a well regulated larder, what I propose may be idle; but
it is particularly useful in the case of game sent weekly
from distant manors."

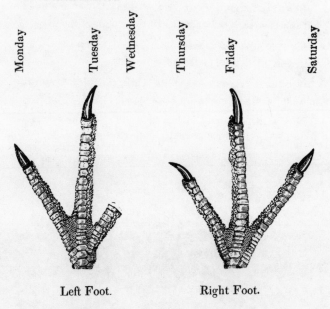

Left Foot.   Right Foot.

N. B. This Bird is supposed to have been killed on a
Wednesday.

THE GOLDEN EAGLE.

(Falco Chrysaëtos, Linnæus.—*Le Grand Aigle,* Buffon.)

THIS is the largest of the genus; it measures from
the point of the bill to the extremity of the tail, upwards of three feet; from tip to tip of the wings, above
eight; weighs from sixteen to eighteen pounds. The

male is smaller, and does not weigh more than twelve
pounds.   The bill is of a deep blue; cere yellow: eyes
large, deep sunk, and covered by a brow projecting;
the iris is of a fine bright yellow, and sparkles with
uncommon lustre.   The general colour is deep brown,
mixed with tawny on the head and neck: quills cho-
colate, with white shafts; tail black spotted with ash:
legs yellow, feathered down to the toes, which are very
scaly; the claws are remarkably large; the middle one
is two inches in length.

   This noble bird is found in various parts of Europe;
but abounds most in the warmer regions, seldom being
met with farther north than the fifty-fifth degree of
latitude.   It is known to breed in the mountainous
parts of Ireland: lays three, and sometimes four eggs,
though it seldom happens that more than two are prolific.   Pennant says there are instances, though rare,
of their having bred in Snowdon Hills.   Wallis, in
his Natural History of Northumberland says, " it formerly had its aerie on the highest and steepest part of
Cheviot.   In the beginning of January, 1735, a very
large one was shot near Warkworth, which measured
from point to point of its wings, eleven feet and a
quarter."

THE OSPREY.

BALD BUZZARD, SEA EAGLE, OR FISHING HAWK.

(Falco Haliaëtus, Linn.—*Le Balbuzzard,* Buff.)

THE length of the male is twenty-two inches, the female about two feet; breadth above five: bill black, cere blue, eye yellow: crown of the head white, marked with oblong dusky spots; the cheeks, and all the under parts of the body, are white, slightly spotted with brown on the breast; from the corner of each eye a streak of dark brown extends down the sides of the neck towards the wing; the upper part of the body is

brown; the two middle tail feathers the same; the
others are marked on the inner webs with alternate
bars of brown and white: legs very short and thick,
being only two inches and a quarter long, and two
inches in circumference; they are of a pale blue;
claws black: outer toe larger than the inner one,
and turns easily backward, by which means this bird
can more readily secure its slippery prey.

Buffon observes that the Osprey is the most numerous of the large birds of prey, and is scattered over
Europe, from Sweden to Greece, and that it is found
even in Egypt and Nigritia.   Its haunts are on the sea
shore, and on the borders of rivers and lakes: its principal food is fish; it darts upon its prey with great
rapidity, and undeviating aim.   The Italians com-
pare its descent upon the water to a piece of lead falling upon that element, aud distinguish it by the name
of *Aquila Piumbina*, or the Leaden Eagle.   It builds
its nest on the ground, among reeds, and lays three
or four eggs, of an elliptical form, rather less than
those of a hen.   The Carolina and Cayenne Ospreys
are varieties of this species.

PEREGRINE FALCON.*

PASSENGER FALCON.

(Falco peregrinus, Linn.—*Le Faucon pelerin,* Buff.)

THIS bird has greatly the look of the Hobby Hawk, but is much larger: length eighteen inches, breadth three feet six and a half inches, weight two and a quarter pounds. The bill is pale blue, tipped with black; it is short, strong, and much notched. The irides are dark; orbits and cere yellow: the head, hinder

---

* The female in falconry is called a *Falcon,* the male a *Tercel;* the female yearling is termed a *red Falcon,* the male a *red Tercel,* and when thoroughly docile is called *Gentle* or *Gentil Hawk.* This is the Lanner of the British Zoology. Captain Sabine includes the Falco communis of Gmelin and the French naturalists, among the synonymes of the Peregrine.

part of the neck, and cheeks, are brownish black, with
a stripe of that colour falling down from the cheeks
and corners of the mouth, before the auriculars, on
each side of the throat. The upper plumage is dingy
bluish ash, more or less clouded and barred with dark
brown, and the shaft of each feather black. The bastard wing, and the primary and secondary quills appear at a first glance to be of an uniform plain dark
ash coloured brown, but on a nearer inspection, the
whole are seen to be barred with darker spots, and
tipped with dull white. The rump and tail coverts
are more distinctly barred, and of a lighter colour
than the other upper parts. The tail, which consists
of twelve feathers, is a dark dingy ash, barred or
spotted with brownish black, and tipped with pale
brown or dirty white. The under parts of the plumage are pale clay colour, plain on the auriculars,
chin, and fore part of the neck; but towards the
breast, the feathers are slightly marked with very small
scratches of black, and the breast with roundish black
spots. The sides, belly, and insides of the wings
are dull white, beautifully and distinctly barred with
dark brown; the primary and secondary quills, on the
inside, are also barred, in the same way, with ash and
dingy freckled white. The thighs are long, and prettily marked with small heart-shaped spots; legs and
toes short, strong and yellow; claws black.

The bird from which this figure and description
were taken, was a male, shot by M. Bell, Esq. of
Woolsington, in the act of tearing a Partridge, March
21, 1814. Length from bill to tail sixteen inches;
breadth thirty-seven inches; weight twenty-three
ounces and a half.

THE KITE

FORK-TAILED KYTE, OR GLEAD.

(Falco Milvus, Linn.—*Le Milan Royal,* Buff.)

Is easily distinguished from the Buzzard, and indeed from all the rest of the tribe, by its forked tail. Its length is about two feet: bill horn colour, furnished with bristles at the base; eyes and cere yellow; the feathers on the head and neck are long and narrow, of a hoary colour, streaked with brown down the middle of each; those on the body are reddish brown, the margin of each feather pale; quills dark brown, legs yellow, claws black. It is common in England, where it continues the whole year. Is found in various parts of Europe, in very northern latitudes, whence it re-

tires towards Egypt before winter, in great numbers:
it is said to breed there, and return in April to Europe, where it breeds a second time, contrary to the
nature of rapacious birds in general. It lays two or
three eggs of a whitish colour, spotted with pale yellow, of a roundish form. Though the Kite weighs
somewhat less than three pounds, the extent of its
wings is more than five feet; its flight is rapid, and it
soars very high in the air, frequently beyond the reach
of sight; yet from this distance descends upon its
prey with irresistible force: its attacks are confined
to small quadrupeds and birds; it is particularly fond
of young chickens, but the fury of their mother is
generally sufficient to drive away the robber.

THE ASH COLOURED FALCON.

(Falco cineraceus, Montagu.)

MONTAGU gives a figure and description of this bird as one hitherto not noticed as a distinct species, and has with his usual minuteness detailed his reasons for thinking it is. The bird is now universally recognized, subsequent observation having amply established the accuracy of the account given by this indefatigable naturalist. He says, " that it has been long known and confounded with the Hen-Harrier, a proof of which is evident by the description of what Pennant supposed a variety of the Ringtail." He adds, " that

it is hardly necessary to remark, that the bright ferruginous colour of the markings is always sufficient to
discriminate this." In the adult male, these bright
markings on the under parts of the body, and under
the wings, and the black bars on the secondary quills,
independent of the great difference in the tail, at once
point out the distinction from the male Hen-Harrier.
In the female, the uniform ferruginous colour of all
the under parts is sufficient to discriminate it from the
female Hen-Harrier, besides the colours being much
brighter : and in the adolescent or changing state of
the plumage, the same difference exists in the markings. These birds breed in the south of England, but
whether they remain with us the whole year, has not
been ascertained. Our figure was from a stuffed specimen obligingly lent to this work by P. J. Selby, of
Twizell House, Esq.

THE HOBBY.

(Falco Subbuteo, Linn.—*Le Hobereau,* Buff.)

THE length of the male is twelve inches; breadth
about two feet; the tips of the wings reach beyond
the extremity of the tail. The bill is blue; cere and
orbits of the eyes yellow; irides orange; a light coloured streak passes over each eye; the top of the
head, and back, are bluish black; wing coverts the
same, but in some edged with rust colour; the hinder
part of the neck is marked with two pale yellow spots;
a black mark from behind each eye, pointing forward,
is extended down on the neck; the breast and belly
are pale, marked with dusky streaks; the thighs rusty,
with long dusky streaks; wings brown; the two middle tail feathers deep dove colour, the others barred

with rusty, and tipped with white; the legs and feet
are yellow.   The female is much larger, and the spots
on her breast more conspicuous than those of the male.

The Hobby breeds with us, lays three or four bluish
white eggs, irregularly spotted with grey and olive,
and is said to emigrate in October.   It was formerly
used in falconry, chiefly for Larks and other small
birds, which were caught in a singular manner: when
the Hawk was cast off, the Larks, fixed to the ground
through fear, became an easy prey to the fowler, who
drew a net over them.   Buffon says, that it was used
in taking Partridges and Quails.

THE SPARROWHAWK.

(*Falco Nisus,* Linn.—*L'Epervier,* Buff.)

LENGTH of the male twelve inches; the female fifteen. The bill is blue, furnished with bristles at the
base, which overhang the nostrils; eye bright orange;
head flat at the top, and above each eye is a strong
bony projection, which seems as if intended to secure
it from external injury: from this projection a few
scattered spots of white form a faint line running backward towards the neck: the top of the head and all
the upper parts are of a dusky brown; on the back
part of the head there is a faint line of white; the scapulars are marked with two spots of white on each feather; the greater quill feathers and the tail are dusky,
with four bars of a darker hue on each; the inner
webs of all the quills are marked with two or more

large white spots; the tips of the tail feathers white; the breast, belly, and under coverts of the wings and thighs are white, beautifully barred with brown; the throat is faintly streaked with brown: legs and feet yellow; claws black.

The above is the description of a female: the male differs both in size and colour: the upper part of his body is of a dark lead colour, and the bars on his breast are more numerous.

The female builds her nest in hollow trees, high rocks, or lofty ruins, sometimes in the old nest of a crow, and generally lays four or five eggs spotted with red at the thicker end.

The Sparrowhawk is very numerous in various parts of the world, from Russia to the Cape of Good Hope. It is a bold and spirited bird; but is obedient and docile, and can be easily trained to hunt Partridges and Quails; it makes great destruction among Pigeons, young poultry, and small birds of all kinds, which it will attack and carry off in the most daring manner.

STONE FALCON.

(Falco Lithofalco, Linn.—*Le Rochier,* Buff.)

THIS rare species, from some of its markings, has
the appearance of a hybrid between the Kestrel and
the Merlin, though differing from both. Our specimen, which was lent to this work by a young friend
and promising naturalist, Mr John Hancock, of Newcastle, is the fourth of the kind which we have ever
heard of in the north of England. Length eleven
and a half inches; breadth twenty-four and three-
quarters; weight six and a half ounces. The bill is
bluish; irides black: its upper plumage is of a deep
lead coloured blue; with each feather on the back,
wing coverts, scapulars, and upper part of the head,
streaked longitudinally at their shafts with black: the
quill feathers are dark brown; inner webs crossed with

bars or spots of white: the end of the tail is broadly
barred with black, tipped with white; the inner webs,
except the two middle feathers, are marked with unde-
fined or indistinct darkish bars or spots; under parts
rufous, with longitudinal brown streaks or spots: the
sides of the neck to the nape are also rufous; and the
cheeks faintly partake of the same colour; the chin
white; legs yellow; claws black.

A doubtful species, or variety of this bird, is quoted
from Buffon by Latham, under the name of the Fal-
coner's Merlin. We have arranged it as the Stone
Falcon, though not wholly satisfied of its identity.
Temminck seems to consider the latter as not a distinct species, but as belonging to some of the stages of
the Merlin.

THE MERLIN.

(Falco Æsalon, Linn.—*L'Emérillon,* Buff.)

THE Merlin is the smallest of the Hawk kind in
this country, scarcely exceeding the size of a Blackbird. The bill is blue; cere and irides yellow: head
rust colour, streaked with black; back and wings of a
deepish brown, tinged with ash, streaked down the
shafts with black, and edged with rusty: quill feathers
dark, tipped and margined on the inner webs with
reddish white; breast and belly yellowish white, with
ferruginous streaks pointing downwards; the tail is
long, and marked with alternate dusky and pale bars;
the wings when closed, do not reach quite to the end
of the tail: legs yellow; claws black.

The Merlin, though small, is not inferior in courage to any of the Falcon tribe. It was used for taking Larks, Partridges, and Quails, which it would frequently kill by one blow, striking them on the breast, head, or neck. Buffon observes that this bird differs from the Falcons, and all the rapacious kind, in the male and female being of the same size. The Merlin does not breed here, but visits us in October; it flies low, and with great celerity and ease. It preys on small birds; breeds in woods, and lays five or six whitish eggs, marbled at the end with greenish brown.

THE EAGLE-OWL,

OR GREAT EARED OWL,

(Strix Bubo, Linn.—*Le Duc, ou Grand Duc,* Buff.)

Is one of the largest of the British Owls, and has a

powerful as well as a dignified look. The tufts or ear
feathers are more than two inches long. The bill is
strong, much hooked, and black; claws the same;
irides reddish yellow; legs very stout, and covered
with a great thickness of short mottled brown feathers;
toes the same down to the claws. The predominant
colours of the plumage are very dark brown and ferruginous, but mixed and beautifully variegated with
markings and shades of black, brown, and yellow,
with spots of white, crossed with zig-zag lines, and
innumerable minute specklings of white, ash-grey, and
brown. The outline of our figure was taken from a
living bird exhibited in a show, the markings of the
plumage from a very ill stuffed specimen, which was
taken on the coast of Norway, and obligingly lent to
this work by Captain Wm Gilchrist, of this port.
This bird is sometimes met with in the northern Scottish isles, where it preys upon Rabbits and Grouse,
which are numerous there, but it is very rarely seen in
England: it generally lays two or three eggs; Temminck says they are white.

THE LONG-EARED OWL.

(Strix Otus, Linn.—*Le Hibou*, Buff.)

LENGTH fourteen inches; breadth about three feet.
The bill is black; irides bright yellow; the radiated
circle round each eye is of a light cream colour, in
some parts tinged with red; between the bill and the
eye there is a circular streak of dark brown; another
circle of dark rusty brown entirely surrounds the face;
its ear tufts consist of six feathers, closely laid together, of a dark brown, tipped and edged with yellow;
the upper part of the body is beautifully penciled with
fine streaks of white, rusty, and brown; the breast
and neck are yellow, finely marked with dusky streaks,

pointing downwards; the belly, thighs, and vent feathers of a light cream colour: there are four or five large white spots upon each wing; the quill and tail feathers are marked with dusky and reddish bars: the legs are feathered down to the claws, which are very sharp; the outer claw is moveable, and may be turned backwards.

This bird is common in various parts of Europe, as well as in this country; its usual haunts are in old ruined buildings, in rocks, and in hollow trees. Buffon observes, that it seldom constructs a nest of its own, but not unfrequently occupies that of the Magpie: it lays four or five white eggs, rounded at the ends; the young are at first white, but acquire their natural colour in about fifteen days.

THE FEMALE SHORT-EARED OWL.

This bird was somewhat larger than the former;
the colours and marks were the same, but much darker, and the spots on the breast larger and more numerous; the ears were not discernible. Being a dead
bird, and having not seen any other at the time, the
editor supposed it to be a distinct kind; but having
since seen several, both males and females, is con-
vinced of the mistake.

Of the Shrike.

THE last family of rapacious birds to be mentioned, is that of the Shrike, which, though they are small, and of a delicate form, yet their courage, their appetite for blood, and their hooked bill entitle them to be ranked with the boldest and the most sanguinary of the rapacious tribe. This genus has been variously placed in the systems of naturalists; it has been classed with the Falcons, with the Pies, and it has even been ranked, especially by the later continental writers, with the harmless and inoffensive tribes of the Passerine kind, to which, indeed, in outward appearance at least, it bears some resemblance. Conformably, however, with what seems to be the most natural arrangement, it is here placed in the rear of those birds which live by rapine and plunder; and, like most of the connecting links in the great chain of nature, it will be found to possess a middle quality, partaking of those which are placed on each side of it, and making thereby an easy transition from the one to the other.

The Shrike genus is distinguished by the following characteristics: the bill is strong, straight at the base, and hooked or bent towards the end; the upper mandible is notched near the tip, and the base furnished with bristles; it has no cere; the tongue is divided at the end, the outer toe connected to the middle one as far as the first joint. To these exterior marks may be added, that it possesses the most undaunted courage, and will attack birds much larger and stronger than itself, such as the Crow, the Magpie, and most of the smaller kinds of Hawks: if any of these should fly near the place of its retreat, the Shrike darts upon the invader with loud cries, and drives it from the nest. The parent birds will sometimes join on such occasions; and there are few birds that will venture to abide the contest. Shrikes will chase all the small birds upon the wing, and sometimes will attack Partridges, and even young hares. Thrushes, Blackbirds, and such like, are their common prey; they fix on them with their talons, split the skull with their bill, and feed on them at leisure.

There are three kinds found in this kingdom, of which the following is the largest.

THE ASH-COLOURED SHRIKE.

GREATER BUTCHER BIRD.

(Lanius Excubitor, Linn.—*La Pie-Grièche grise,* Buff.)

THE length about ten inches. Its bill is black, and
furnished with bristles at the base : the upper parts of
its plumage pale blue ash; under parts white; a black
stripe passes through each eye; the greater quills are
black, with a large white spot at the base, forming a
bar of that colour across the wing; the lesser quills
are white at the tips; the scapulars white; the two
middle feathers of the tail black; the next on each
side are white at the ends, gradually increasing to the
outermost, which are nearly all white; the whole,
when the tail is spread, forms a large oval spot of
black; the legs are black. The female differs little
from the male; she lays six eggs, of a dull olive green,
spotted at the end with black.

This bird is rarely found in the cultivated parts of
the country, preferring mountainous wilds, among
furze and thorny thickets. Buffon says it is common
in France, where it continues all the year: it is met
with likewise in Russia, and various parts of Europe;
it preys on small birds, which it seizes by the throat,
and, after strangling, fixes them on a sharp thorn,
and tears them in pieces with its bill. Pennant observes, that when kept in the cage, it sticks its food
against the wires before it will eat it. It is said to imitate the notes of the smaller singing birds, thereby
drawing them near its haunts, in order more securely
to seize them.

The foregoing figure and description were taken
from a very fine specimen, for which this work is indebted to the late Major H. F. Gibson, of the 4th
dragoons.

THE CROW

CARRION CROW, BLACK-NEBBED OR MIDDEN CROW.

(*Corvus Corone*, Linn.—*La Corneille noire*, Buff.)

Is similar to the Raven in its habits, colour, and external appearance.   Length about eighteen inches; breadth three feet.   The glossy feathers of the upper plumage have a burnished look, excepting on their edges, which are dull, and form a border to each. This species is more numerous and as widely spread as the Raven; they live mostly in woods; build their nests in trees; and lay five or six eggs, much like those of the Raven.   They feed on putrid flesh, and garbage of all sorts; likewise on eggs, shell fish, worms, and insects.

These wary birds live in pairs, and are commonly seen together flying at a great height, out of the
reach of the gun, while they are prowling over the
country in search of their food, which, with pene-
trating eye, and acute scent, they discover afar off.
They pluck the feathers off the dead birds, toss them
aside, and then pick the flesh from the bones.   In
winter they take shelter from the extremity of the
weather, in the hollows of rocky precipices.

THE ROOK

(Corvus frugilegus, Linn.—*Le Freux*, Buff.)

Is about the size of the Carrion Crow, and in its figure
very much resembles it. The base of the bill and
nostrils, as far as the eyes, is covered with a rough
scabrous skin, in which it differs from all the rest
of the genus, caused, it is said, by thrusting its bill
into the earth in search of worms,* but as the same
appearance has been observed in such as have been
brought up tame and unaccustomed to that mode of

---

* It is curious to observe the effectual method they take to secure
their prey entire; they first seize the worm by the head, and pull it
out as far as they can, so as not to break it, and then place their foot
upon this part, till they can safely extricate the whole from its hole
in the earth.

subsistence, we are inclined to consider it an original peculiarity. Rooks are fond of the erucæ of the hedge-chafer, or chesnut brown beetle,* for which they search with indefatigable pains. They are often accused of feeding on the corn just after it has been sown, and various contrivances have been made both to kill and frighten them away; but, in our estimation, the advantages derived from the destruction which they make among grubs, larvæ, worms, and noxious insects, greatly overpay the injury done to the future harvest, by the small quantity of corn they may destroy in searching after their favourite food. They are gregarious, and fly in immense flocks morning and evening to and from their roosting places in quest of food. During the breeding time they are jealous and watchful, and will rob each other when they can. They live together in large societies, and build close to each other in trees, frequently in the midst of large and populous towns. These rookeries, however, are often the scenes of bitter contests; the new-comers are frequently driven away by the old inhabitants, their half-built nests torn in pieces, and the unfortunate couple forced to begin their work anew in

* These insects appear in hot weather, in formidable numbers, disrobing the fields and trees of their verdure, blossoms, and fruit, spreading desolation and destruction wherever they go. They appeared in great numbers in Ireland during a hot summer, and committed great ravages. In the year 1747, whole meadows and corn fields were destroyed by them in Suffolk. The decrease of rookeries in that county was thought to be the occasion of it. The many rookeries with us is in some measure the reason why we have so few of these destructive insects.

Wallis's History of Northumberland.

some more undisturbed situation : of this we had a remarkable instance in Newcastle.   In the year 1783, a
pair of Rooks, after an unsuccessful attempt to esta-
blish themselves in a rookery at no great distance from
the Exchange, were compelled to abandon the attempt.
They took refuge on the spire of that building, and although constantly interrupted by other Rooks, built
their nest on the top of the vane, and brought forth
their young, undisturbed by the noise of the populace
below them; the nest and its inhabitants turning about
with every change of the wind.   They returned and
built their nest every year on the same place till 1793,
soon after which the spire was taken down.

THE JACK-DAW.

(Corvus Monedula, Linn.—*Le Choucas,* Buff.)

THIS bird is considerably less than the Rook, being
only thirteen inches in length, and about twenty-eight
in breadth. The bill is black: eyes white; the hinder
part of the head and neck hoary grey; the rest of the
plumage is of a fine glossy black above; beneath
dusky; the legs are black.

The Daw is very common in England, and remains
with us the whole year: in other countries, as France
and various parts of Germany, it is migratory. They
frequent churches, old towers, and ruins, in great
flocks, where they build: the female lays five or six
eggs, paler than those of the Crow, and smaller.
They rarely build in trees: in Hampshire they some-

times breed in rabbit holes.*   They are easily tamed,
and may be taught to pronounce several words: they
will conceal part of their food, and with it small pieces
of money, or toys.   They feed on insects, grain, fruit,
and small pieces of flesh, and will also eat eggs.

There is a variety of the Daw found in Switzerland,
having a white collar round its neck.   In Norway and
even in this country, individuals have been seen perfectly white.

* White's Natural History of Selborne.

THE MAGPIE.

PIANET.

(Corvus Pica, Linn.—*La Pie,* Buff.)

LENGTH about eighteen inches. Bill strong and
black; eyes hazel; head, neck, back, breast, and tail
coverts deep black, forming a fine contrast with the
snowy whiteness of the under parts and scapulars; the
neck feathers are long, as are also those on the back,
which extend towards the rump, leaving only a small
space, of ash-grey, between them and the tail coverts;
the plumage in general is glossed with green, purple,
and blue, which catch the eye in different lights, and
are particularly resplendent on the tail, which is very
long, and rather wedge-shaped; vent, under tail-co-
verts, thighs, and legs black: on the throat and part

of the neck the feathers are mixed with others, resembling strong whitish hairs.

This bird is every where common in England; and
is likewise found in various parts of the Continent, but
not so far north as Lapland, nor farther south than
Italy: it is met with in America, but not commonly,
and is migratory there. Like the Crow it is omnivo-
rous. They make their nest with great art, leaving a
hole in the side for admittance, and covering the whole
upper part with an interweaving of thorny twigs, closely entangled, thereby securing a retreat from the rude
attacks of other birds: the inside is furnished with a
sort of mattrass, composed of wool and other soft materials, on which the young repose: the female lays
seven or eight eggs, pale green, spotted with black.

The Magpie is crafty and familiar, and may be
taught to pronounce words, and even short sentences,
and will imitate any particular noise. It is addicted,
like other birds of its kind, to stealing and hoarding.
It is smaller than the Jackdaw, and its wings are
shorter in proportion; accordingly its flight is not so
lofty, nor so well sustained: it never undertakes long
journies, but flies only from tree to tree, at moderate
distances.

THE JAY.

(Corvus glandarius, Linn.—*Le Geai,* Buff.)

THIS beautiful bird is not more than thirteen inches
in length. Its bill is black; eyes white; the feathers
on the forehead are white, streaked with black, and
form a tuft which it can erect and depress at pleasure;
the chin is white, and from the corners of the bill on
each side proceeds a broad streak of black, which passes under the eye; the hinder part of the head, the
neck, and back, are of a cinnamon colour; breast the
same, but lighter; lesser wing coverts bay; the belly
and vent almost white; the greater wing coverts are
elegantly barred with black, fine pale blue, and white
alternately; the greater quills are black, with pale
edges, the bases of some of them white; lesser quills

black; those next the body chesnut; the rump is white; tail black, with pale brown edges; legs dirty pale brown.

The Jay is common in Great Britain, and is found in various parts of Europe. It is distinguished as well for the beautiful arrangement of its colours, as for its harsh, grating voice, and restless disposition. Upon seeing the sportsman, it gives, by its cries, the alarm of danger. It builds in woods, and makes an artless nest, composed of sticks, fibres, and slender twigs: lays five or six eggs, ash grey, mixed with green, and faintly spotted with brown. Pennant observes, that the young ones continue with their parents till the following spring, when they separate to form new pairs.

They live on acorns, nuts, seeds, and fruits; will eat eggs, and sometimes destroy young birds in the absence of the old ones. When domesticated, they may be rendered very familiar, and will imitate a variety of words and sounds. We have heard one imitate the sound of a saw so exactly, that though it was on a Sunday, we could hardly be persuaded that there was not a carpenter at work in the house. Another, at the approach of cattle, had learned to hound a cur dog upon them, by whistling and calling his name: at last, during frost, the dog was excited to attack a cow big with calf, when the animal fell on the ice, and was hurt: the Jay was complained of as a nuisance, and its owner was obliged to destroy it. They sometimes assemble in great numbers early in the spring, and seem to hold a conference, probably, for the purpose of fixing upon the districts they are to occupy: to hear them is truly curious; while some gabble, shout, or whistle, others with a raucous voice, seem to command attention: the noise made on these occasions may be aptly compared to that of a distant meeting of disorderly drunken persons.

THE CHATTERER.

SILK TAIL, OR WAXEN CHATTERER.

(Ampelis Garrulus, Linn.—*Le Jaseur de Boheme*, Buff.)

THIS beautiful bird is about eight inches in length.
Its bill is black, and has a small notch at the end; the
eyes, which are black and shining, are placed in a band
of black, passing from the base of the bill to the
hinder part of the head; throat black; the feathers
on the head long, forming a crest; all the upper parts
of the body are of a reddish ash; breast and belly inclining to purple; the vent and tail coverts in some,
nearly white; in others, the former reddish chesnut,
the latter ash grey: the tail feathers are black, tipped
with pale yellow; the quills black, the third and fourth
tipped on their outer edges with white, the five follow-

ing with straw colour, but in some bright yellow; the secondaries are tipped with white, each being pointed with a flat horny substance of a bright vermillion. These appendages vary in different subjects; one in our possession, had eight on one wing and six on the other. The legs are short and black. The female has only four or five of the second quills tipt with the red cartilaginous appendages, and the young birds previous to their first moult are without them altogether.

This rare bird visits our island only at uncertain intervals. In the years 1790, 1791, and 1803, several were taken in Northumberland and Durham, in the month of November. Their summer residence is the northern parts of Europe, within the arctic circle, whence they spread themselves into other countries, where they remain during winter, and return in the spring to their usual haunts. Their general food is berries and insects: one which we saw in a state of captivity was fed chiefly with hawthorn and ivy berries, but from the difficulty of providing it with this food, it soon died. Its breeding place is not well ascertained. Only this species of the Chatterer is recognised as a British bird; the same may be said of the two genera next in succession.

THE STARLING.

STARE.

(Sturnus vulgaris, Linn.—*L'Etourneau,* Buff.)

LENGTH somewhat less than nine inches. The bill is straight, sharp-pointed, and of a yellowish brown; in old birds deep yellow; the nostrils are surrounded by a prominent rim; the eyes are brown; the whole plumage dark, glossed with green, blue, purple, and copper, but each feather is marked at the end with a pale yellow spot; the wing coverts are edged with yellowish brown; the quill and tail feathers dusky, with light edges: the legs are reddish brown.

From the striking similarity, both in form and man-

ners, observable in the Starling, and those more immediately preceding, we have no scruple in removing it
from the usual place, as it evidently forms a connecting link between them, and in a variety of points seems
equally allied to both. Few birds are more generally
known than the Starling, it being an inhabitant of almost every climate; and as it is a familiar bird, and
easily trained in a state of captivity, its habits have
been more frequently observed than those of most
other birds. They make an artless nest in the hollows
of trees, rocks, or old walls, and sometimes in cliffs
overhanging the sea: lay four or five eggs, of a pale
greenish ash: the young are dusky brown till the first
moult. In the autumn they fly in vast flocks, and may
be known at a great distance, by their whirling mode
of flight, which Buffon compares to a sort of vortex,
in which the collective body performs an uniform circular revolution, and at the same time continues to
make a progressive advance. The evening is the time
when the Starlings assemble in the greatest numbers,
and, it is said, betake themselves to the fens and
marshes, where they roost among the reeds: they
chatter much in the evening and morning, both when
they assemble and disperse. So attached are they to
society, that they not only join those of their own species, but also birds of a different kind, and are frequently seen in company with Redwings, Fieldfares,
and even with Crows, Jackdaws, and Pigeons. Their
principal food consists of worms, snails, and caterpillars; they likewise break and suck the eggs of other
birds, and eat various kinds of grain, seeds, and berries, and are said to be particularly fond of cherries.

In a confined state they eat small pieces of raw flesh,
bread soaked in water, &c. are very docile, and may
easily be taught to repeat short phrases, or whistle
tunes with great exactness, and are capable of imitating the notes of other birds. In pairing time they
are extremely frolicsome, flapping, fluttering, and
hurrying around and over each other, with odd gestures and tones.

THE REDWING

SWINEPIPE, OR WIND THRUSH,

(*Turdus Iliacus*, Linn.—*Le Mauvis*, Buff.)

Is about eight inches in length. Bill dark brown;
eyes deep hazel; plumage in general similar to that of
the Thrush, but a white streak over the eye distin-
guishes it from that bird; belly not quite so much
spotted, sides of the body and the feathers under the
wings tinged with red, which is its peculiar characteristic; whence also its name.

These birds make their appearance a few days before the Fieldfare,* and are generally seen with them

---

* A Redwing was taken up November 7th, 1785, at six o'clock in
the morning, which, on its approach to land, had flown against the
light-house at Tynemouth, and was so stunned that it fell to the
ground and died soon after; the light most probably had attracted
its attention.

after their arrival; they frequent the same places, eat
the same food, and are very similar to them in manners. Like the Fieldfare, they leave us in the spring,
for which reason their song is almost unknown to us,
but it is said to be very pleasing. In Sweden they
perch on high trees in the forests, and have a fine note
in the breeding season. The female builds her nest in
low bushes or hedges, and lays six eggs, of a greenish
blue colour, spotted with black.*

* This and the former are delicate eating : the Romans held them
in such estimation that they kept thousands of them together in aviaries, and fed them with a sort of paste made of bruised figs and
flour, and various other kind of food, to improve the delicacy and
flavour of their flesh : these aviaries were so contrived as to admit
light barely sufficient to direct them to their food; every object
which might tend to remind them of their former liberty was carefully kept out of sight, such as the fields, the woods, the birds, or
whatever might disturb the repose necessary to their improvement.
Under this management these birds fattened, to the great profit of
their proprietors, who sold them to the Roman epicures for three de-
narii, or about two shillings sterling each.

THE BLACKBIRD.

BLACK OUZEL.

(Turdus Merula, Linn.—*Le Merle,* Buff.)

THE length of the Blackbird is generally about ten
inches. Its plumage is altogether black; the bill, inside of the mouth, and edges of the eye-lids are yellow,
as are also the soles of the feet; legs dirty yellow. The
female is mostly deep brown, inclining to rust colour
on the breast and belly; bill dusky, legs brown; her
song is also very different, so that she has sometimes
been mistaken for a bird of a different species.

The males, during the first year, resemble the females so much as not easily to be distinguished from
them; but after that, they assume the yellow bill, and
other distinguishing marks of their sex. The Blackbird is a solitary bird, frequenting woods and thickets,

chiefly evergreens, especially where there are perennial
springs, which together afford it both shelter and subsistence.   They feed on berries, fruits, insects, and
worms; but never fly in flocks like Thrushes; they
pair early, and begin to warble nearly as soon as
any other songsters of the grove.   They build in
bushes or low trees, and lay four or five eggs, of a
bluish green, marked irregularly with dusky spots.
The young birds are easily tamed, and may be taught
to whistle a variety of tunes.   They are restless and
timorous birds, easily alarmed, and difficult of access;
but they readily suffer themselves to be caught with
bird-lime, nooses, and all sorts of snares.   They
are never kept in aviaries, but generally in cages
apart; for, when shut up with other birds, they pursue and harass their companions unceasingly.   In
some counties of England this bird is called simply
the Ouzel.

THE RING OUZEL.

(Turdus torquatus, Linn.—Le Merle à Plastron Blanc,
Buff.)

THIS bird very much resembles the Blackbird: its
general colour is dull black; each feather margined
with ash grey; the bill is dusky; corners of the mouth
and inside yellow; eyes hazel; the breast is distinguished by a crescent of pure white, which almost surrounds the neck, and from which it derives its name:
the legs are dusky brown. The female differs in having the crescent on the breast much less conspicuous,
and, in some birds, wholly wanting, which has caused
some authors to consider it as a different species, under the name of the Rock Ouzel.

Ring Ouzels are found in various parts of this kingdom, chiefly in the wilder and more mountainous districts: with this exception, their habits are similar to

those of the Blackbird; the female builds her nest
in the same manner, and in similar situations, and
lays four or five eggs of the same colour: they feed
on insects and berries of various kinds, are fond of
grapes, and Buffon, observes, during the season of
vintage are generally fat, and at that time are
esteemed delicious eating. The same author says,
that in France they are migratory.   In some parts
of this kingdom they have been observed to change
places, particularly in Hampshire, where they are
known generally to stay not more than a fortnight at
one time. The foregoing representation was taken
from one killed near Bedlington, Northumberland.

THE BLACK WOODPECKER.

(*Picus martius*, Linn.—*Le Pic noir*, Buff.)

THIS scarce bird is the largest of the British Wood-
peckers, being about seventeen inches in length, bill
nearly two and a half, of a horn colour, and pale yellow on the sides; irides also pale yellow; the crown
of the head is crimson, and the feathers elongated to
the nape; the quills are brown, and all the rest of the
plumage dull black; the legs are lead grey, having
the fore part covered with feathers half their length.

The female differs from the male, the hinder part
of her head only being red, and in some specimens,
the red is entirely wanting; the black parts of her
plumage are also duller.　They form their nest in the
deep hollows of old trees, and like the rest of the
genus lay two or three white eggs.

THE NUTHATCH.

NUTJOBBER, WOODCRACKER.

(Sitta europea, Linn.—*La Sittelle ou le Torchepot,*
Buff.)

THE length is near six inches; bill strong, black
above, beneath almost white; the eyes hazel; a black
stroke passes over each eye, from the bill, extending
down the side of the neck as far as the shoulder; all
the upper part of the body is of a fine blue grey; the
cheeks and chin white; breast and belly of a pale
orange; sides marked with streaks of chesnut; quills
dusky; the tail is short, the two middle feathers grey,
the rest dusky, three of the outermost spotted with
white; legs pale yellow; claws large, sharp, and much

bent, the back claw very strong; when extended the foot measures one inch and three quarters.

This, like the Woodpecker, frequents woods, and is a shy and solitary bird: the female lays her eggs, which are white, with a few pale brown spots, in holes of trees, frequently in those which have been deserted by the Woodpecker. The nest is fitted up with layers of the very thin flakes or laminæ of the bark of the Scotch fir. During the time of incubation, she is easily driven from her nest, and on being disturbed, hisses like a snake. The Nuthatch feeds on caterpillars, beetles, and various kinds of insects; it likewise eats nuts, and from its expertness in cracking them has obtained its name: having placed a nut fast in a chink, it takes its stand a little above, and striking it with all its force, perforates the shell and picks out the kernel; when disturbed at its work, it very readily removes the nut and flies away with it. In the same way it also breaks into the very hard shells of the stone pine. Like the Woodpecker, it moves up and down the trunks of trees with great facility, in search of food. It does not migrate, but in the winter approaches nearer inhabited places, is sometimes seen in orchards and gardens, and is fond of picking bones.

THE GROSBEAK.

HAWFINCH.

(Loxia Coccothraustes, Linn.—*Le Gros-bec,* Buff.)

LENGTH nearly seven inches. Bill of a horn colour, conical, and prodigiously thick at the base; eyes ash grey; the space between the bill and the eye, and thence to the chin and throat, is black; the top of the head reddish chesnut, as are also the cheeks, but somewhat paler, back part of the neck greyish ash; the back and lesser wing coverts chesnut; the greater wing coverts grey, in some almost white, forming a band across the wing; the quills are all black, excepting some of the secondaries nearest the body, which are brown; the four outer quills seem as if clipped off at the ends; the primaries have each a spot of white about the middle of the inner web; breast and belly pale rusty, fading almost to white at the vent; the tail is black, excepting the ends of the middle feathers, which are grey; the outer ones are tipped with white; legs pale brown. The female greatly resembles the male, but her colours are less vivid, and the space between the bill and the eye is grey instead of black. These birds vary considerably, as scarcely two of them are alike: in some the head is wholly black: in others the whole upper part of the body is of that colour; and others have been met with entirely white, excepting the wings.

This species is an inhabitant of the temperate climates, from Spain, Italy, and France, as far as Sweden, but visits this island only occasionally, and generally in winter, when it is probably driven over in its passage from its northern haunts to the milder climates of France and Italy. It breeds in those countries, but is no where numerous. Buffon says it is a shy and solitary bird, with little or no song; it generally inhabits the woods during summer, and in winter resorts near the hamlets and farms. The female builds her nest in trees, of small dry roots and grass, lined with warmer materials. The eggs are roundish, bluish green, spotted with brown. She feeds her young with insects, chrysalids, and other soft nutritious substances.

THE YELLOW BUNTING.

YELLOW HAMMER, OR YELLOW YOWLEY.

(Emberiza Citrinella, Linn.—*Le Bruant,* Buff.)

LENGTH somewhat above six inches. Bill dusky; eyes hazel; the prevailing colour is yellow, mixed with brown of various shades; the crown of the head in general, is bright yellow, more or less variegated with brown; the cheeks, throat, and lower part of the belly pure yellow; the breast reddish, and the sides dashed with streaks of the same; the hinder part of the neck and back are greenish olive; the greater quills dusky, edged with pale yellow; lesser quills and scapulars dark brown, edged with grey; the tail is dusky, and a little forked, the feathers edged with light brown, the outermost with white; the legs yellowish brown. It is somewhat difficult to describe a species of bird of which no two are to be found perfectly similar, but its specific characters are plain, and cannot easily be mistaken. The colours of the female are less bright than those of the male, with very little yellow about the head.

This bird is common in every lane and hedge, flitting before the traveller as he passes along, or uttering its simple and frequently repeated monotone. It feeds on various kinds of seeds, insects, &c. The female makes an artless nest, composed of hay, dried roots, and moss, lined with hair and wool: she lays four or five eggs, marked with dark irregular streaks, and frequently has more than one brood in the season. In Italy, where small birds of almost every description are made use of for the table, this is esteemed very good eating, and is frequently fattened for that purpose like the Ortolan; but with us, who are accustomed to grosser kinds of food, it is considered too insignificant to form any part of our repasts.

THE TAWNY BUNTING.*

GREAT PIED MOUNTAIN FINCH, OR BRAMBLING.

(*Emberiza mustelina,* Gm. Linn.)

LENGTH somewhat above six inches. Bill short, yellow, and blackish at the point; crown of the head tawny; forehead chesnut; hinder part of the neck and cheeks the same, but paler; throat, sides of the neck, and space round the eyes dirty white; breast dull yellow; under parts white, in some tinged with yellow; the back and scapulars black, edged with reddish brown; quill feathers dusky, edged with white; secondaries white on the outer edges; greater coverts tipped

---

* In our former editions this bird has been described as a distinct species. Almost all naturalists, however, now agree in considering it "the Snow Bunting" varied by age, sex, climate, or season.

with white, which, when the wing is closed, forms a
bed upon it; upper tail coverts yellow; tail a little
forked, the two outermost feathers white, the third
black, tipped with white, the rest wholly black; legs
short and black; hinder claws almost as long, but more
bent than those of the Lark. The foregoing figure
and description were taken from a bird which was
caught in the high moory grounds above Shotley-
Kirk, Northumberland.

Of the Finch.

THE transition from the Bunting to the Finch is
very easy, and the shade of difference between them,
in some instances, almost imperceptible; on which account they have been frequently confounded with each
other. The principal difference consists in the beak,
which, in the Finch is conical, very thick at the base,
and tapering to a sharp point: in this respect it more
nearly resembles the Grosbeak. Of this family many
are distinguished as well for the liveliness of their song,
as for the beauty and variety of their plumage, on
which account they are much esteemed. They are
very numerous, and assemble sometimes in immense
flocks, feeding on various kinds of seeds and grain, as
well as on insects and their eggs.

THE GOLDFINCH.

GOLDSPINK, OR THISTLE-FINCH.

(Fringilla Carduelis, Linn.—*Le Chardonneret,* Buff.)

THE bill is white, tipped with black; the forehead
and chin a rich scarlet, which is divided by a black line
passing from each corner of the bill to the eyes, which
are dark; the cheeks are white; top of the head black,
which colour extends downward from the nape on
each side, dividing the white on the cheeks from the
white spot on the hinder part of the neck; the back
and rump are cinnamon brown; the sides the same,
but paler; belly white; lesser wing coverts black;
quills black, marked in the middle of each feather with
yellow, forming, when the wing is closed, a large patch;
the tips white; the tail feathers are black, with a white
spot on each near the end; legs pale flesh red.

Beauty of plumage, says the lively Count de Buffon,
melody of song, sagacity, and docility of disposition,

seem all united in this charming little bird, which, were
it rare, and imported from a foreign country, would be
more highly valued. Goldfinches begin to sing early
in the spring, and continue till the time of breeding is
over; when kept in a cage, they will sing the greater
part of the year. In a state of confinement they are
much attached to their keepers, and will learn a variety
of little tricks, such as to draw up small buckets containing their water and food, to fire a cracker, and such
like. They construct a neat and compact nest, which
is composed of moss, dried grass, and roots, lined with
wool, hair, the down of thistles, and other soft and delicate substances. The female lays five white eggs,
marked at the larger end with spots of deep purple.
They feed their young with caterpillars and insects;
the old birds feed on various kinds of seeds, particularly those of the thistle, and occasionally on the seeds
of the Scotch fir.

Goldfinches breed with the Canary; this intermix-
ture succeeds best between the cock Goldfinch and the
hen Canary, whose offspring are productive, and are
said to resemble the male in the shape of the bill, and
in the colours of the head and wings, and the hen in
the rest of the body.

THE LINNET.

BROWN OR GREY LINNET.

(Fringilla Linota, Linn.—*La Linotte,* Buff.)

LENGTH about five inches and a half. The bill bluish grey; eyes hazel; upper parts of the head, the neck, and back, dark reddish brown, edges of the feathers pale; under parts dirty reddish white; breast deeper than the rest, sides streaked with brown; quills dusky, edged with white; tail brown, likewise with white edges, except the two middle feathers, which have reddish margins; it is somewhat forked: legs short and brown. The female is marked on the breast with streaks of brown; she has less white on her wings, and her colours in general are less bright.

This bird is very well known, being common in every part of Europe; and is met with chiefly on moory grounds: it builds its nest concealed in furze bushes; the outside is made up of dry grass, roots, and moss; it is lined with hair and wool. The female lays four or five eggs, they are white, tinged with blue, and irregularly spotted with brown at the larger end: she breeds generally twice in the year. The song of the Linnet is lively and sweetly varied; its manners are gentle, and its disposition docile; it easily adopts the song of other birds, when confined with them, and in some instances it has been taught to pronounce words with great distinctness; but this substitution of imperfect and forced accents, which have neither charms nor beauty, in the room of the free and varied modulations of uninstructed nature, is a perversion of its talents. Linnets are frequently found in flocks: during winter, they feed on various seeds, and are particularly fond of lintseed, from which circumstance, it is said, they derive their name.

THE SPOTTED FLYCATCHER.

BEAM BIRD.

(Muscicapa Grisola, Linn.—*Le Gobe·mouche*, Buff.)

LENGTH nearly five inches and three quarters: bill broad, flatted, and wide at the base, where it is beset with a few short bristles; a ridge runs along the upper mandible; both that and the under one are dusky at the tips, the latter is yellowish towards the base; inside of the mouth yellow: all the upper plumage is of a mouse colour, darkest on the wings and tail: head and neck more or less obscurely spotted with dark brown; the wing coverts, secondary quills, and scapulars, also dark brown, edged with dingy white; under parts very pale ash, or lint coloured white, tinged with rufous on the sides and breast, which latter is marked with streaks of brown: the legs are short, and darkish.

The Flycatcher, of all our summer birds, is the most
mute. It visits this island in the spring, and disap-
pears in September. The female builds her nest commonly in gardens, on any projecting stone in a wall,
or on the end of a beam, screened by the leaves of a
vine, sweet-brier, or woodbine, and sometimes close
to the post of a door, where people are going in and
out all day long. The nest is rather carelessly made;
it is composed chiefly of moss and dried grass, mixed
in the inside with some wool, and a few hairs. She
lays four or five eggs, of a dull white, closely spotted
and blotched with rusty red. This bird feeds on insects, for which it sits watching on a branch or on a
post, suddenly dropping down upon them, and catching them on the wing, and immediately rising, returns
again to its station to wait for more. After the young
have quitted the nest, the parent birds follow them
from tree to tree, and watch them with the most sedu-
lous attention. They feed them with the flies which
flutter among the boughs beneath; or pursuing their
insect prey with a quick irregular kind of flight, like
that of a butterfly, to a greater distance, they immediately return as before described.

THE LARK.

SKY LARK OR LAVROCK.

(Alauda arvensis, Linn.—*L' Alouette,* Buff.)

LENGTH nearly seven inches. Bill dusky, under
mandible somewhat yellow; eyes hazel; over each eye
a pale streak, which extends to the bill, and round the
eye on the under side; on the upper parts of the body
the feathers are of a reddish brown colour, dark in the
middle, with pale edges; the fore part of the neck is
reddish white, spotted with brown; breast, belly, and
thighs white; the quills brown, with pale edges; tail
the same, and somewhat forked, the two middle feathers
darkest, the outermost white on the outer edge; the legs
dusky. In some of our specimens the feathers on the
top of the head were long, and formed a sort of crest
behind. The Lesser Crested Lark of Pennant and
Latham is perhaps only a variety of this bird.

The Lark begins its song* very early in spring, and is heard chiefly in the morning. Shakespeare thus beautifully describes its rising—

> Lo! hear the gentle Lark, weary of rest
> From his moist cabinet mounts up on high,
> And wakes the morning, from whose silver breast
> The sun ariseth in his majesty.

It rises in the air almost perpendicularly and by successive springs, and hovers at a vast height; its descent, on the contrary, is in an oblique direction, unless it is threatened by birds of prey, or attracted by its mate, and on these occasions it drops like a stone. It makes its nest on the ground, between two clods of earth, and lines it with dried grass and roots : the female lays four or five eggs, of a greyish brown, marked with darker spots; she generally has two broods in the year, and sits only about fifteen days. As soon as the young have escaped from the nest, the attachment of the parent seems to increase; she flutters over their heads, directs all their motions, and is ever ready to screen them from danger.

The Lark is diffused almost universally throughout Europe; it is every where extremely prolific, and in some places the prodigious numbers that are frequently caught are truly astonishing. In Germany there is

* Its note is thus quaintly imitated in Sylvester's Du Bartas—

> The pretty Lark, climbing the welkin clear,
> Chaunts with a *cheer, here, peer,* I *near* my *dear ;*
> Then stooping thence, seeming her fall to rue,
> Adieu (she saith) *adieu, dear, dear, adieu.*

an excise upon them, which has produced, according
to Keysler, the sum of 6000 dollars in one year to the
city of Leipsic alone.   Pennant says, the neighbourhood of Dunstable is famous for the great numbers of
these birds found there, and that 4000 dozen have
been taken between September and February, for the
London markets.*   Yet, notwithstanding the great
havoc made among these birds, they are extremely
numerous.   The winter is deemed the best season for
taking them, as they are then very fat, being almost
constantly on the ground, feeding in great flocks;
whereas in summer they are very lean; they then always go in pairs, eat sparingly, and sing incessantly
while on the wing.

* We must here dismiss the disgusting task of noting the edible
qualities of these tiny creatures, the ornament of our fields, our gardens, and groves; nor can we help regarding their destruction for
the purposes of gormandism, as not a little reproachful to humanity,
in countries abounding with every species of food fit for the use of
man.

THE WOODLARK.

(Alauda arborea, Linn.—*L'Alouette de bois,* Buff.)

THIS bird is somewhat smaller than the Field Lark:
the colours of its plumage are much the same, but on
the upper parts paler, and not so distinctly defined: a
white streak passes from the bill over each eye nearly
to the nape; the under parts are white, tinged with
yellow on the throat, and red on the breast, and spotted with black.   The tail is shorter than that of other
Larks, which gives this bird a less tall and slender
shape: the legs are dull yellow; the hinder claw very
long, and somewhat curved.

The Woodlark is generally found near the borders
of woods, from which it derives its name; it perches on
trees, and sings during the night, so as sometimes to be
mistaken for the Nightingale; it likewise sings as it

flies, and builds its nest on the ground, similar to that
of the Skylark. The female lays five eggs, of a dusky
hue, marked with brown spots. It builds very early,
the young, in some seasons, being able to fly about the
latter end of March. It makes two nests in the year,
like the Skylark, but is not nearly so numerous as that
bird.

THE GREY WAGTAIL,

(Motacilla Boarula, Linn.—*La Bergeronette jaune,*
Buff.)

Is somewhat longer than the last. Bill dark brown;
over each eye a pale streak; head, neck, and back ash
grey; throat and chin black; rump and under parts
bright yellow; wing coverts and quills dark brown, the
former with pale edges; tertials, almost as long as
the greater quills, white at the base, and edged with
yellow on the outer webs; middle tail feathers black,
outer one white: legs yellowish brown.

The habits of this bird are similar to those of the
last. It builds on the ground, and sometimes on the
banks of rivulets, laying six or eight eggs, of a dirty
white, with yellow spots. The female has no black
on the throat.

Of the Warblers.

THIS very numerous family is composed of a great
variety of kinds, differing in size from the Nightingale
to the Wren, and not a little in their habits and manners.   They are widely dispersed over most parts of
the world; some of them remain with us during the
whole year;   others are migratory, and visit us annually in great numbers, forming a very considerable
portion of those numerous tribes of singing birds, with
which this island so plentifully abounds.   Some are
distinguished by their flight, which they perform by
jerks, and in an undulating manner;   others by the
whirring motion of their wings.   The head in general
is small;   the bill weak and slender, and beset with
bristles at the base;   the nostrils are small and somewhat depressed;   and the outer toe is joined to the middle one by a small membrane.

THE REDBREAST.

ROBIN-REDBREAST, OR RUDDOCK.

(Motacilla rubecula, Linn.—*Le Rouge Gorge,* Buff.)

THIS general favourite is too well known to need a
very minute description. The bill is slender and delicate ; its eyes large, black, and expressive, and its
aspect mild ; the head and all the upper parts are
brown, tinged with greenish olive; neck and breast of
a fine deep reddish orange; a spot of the same colour
marks its forehead; belly and vent dull white: legs dusky.

In spring the Redbreast retires to woods and thickets,
where, with its mate, it prepares for the accommodation
of its future family. During summer it is rarely to be seen.
The nest is placed near the ground, by the roots of trees.
in the most concealed spot, and sometimes in old buildings, and is constructed of moss and dried leaves, in-
termixed with hair, and lined with feathers : in order

more effectually to conceal it, they cover it over with leaves, leaving only a narrow winding entrance under the heap. The female lays from five to nine eggs, of a dull white, marked with reddish spots. During the time of incubation, the male sits at no great distance, and makes the woods resound with his delightful warble; he keenly chases all the birds of his own species, and drives them from his little settlement; for it has never been known that two pairs of these birds, who are as faithful as they are amorous, were lodged at the same time in the same bush.* The Redbreast prefers the thick shade, where there is water; it feeds on insects and worms; but never eats them alive. It takes them in its bill and beats them against the ground till they cease to move: during this operation it frequently happens that the caterpillar is burst, and its entrails are shaken out, leaving only the body thus cleansed from all its impurities. Some ornithologists have ascribed this to the extreme delicacy of the bird in preparing its repast; others think that it is only an accidental consequence arising from the manner of putting its prey to death.

Although the Redbreast never quits this island, it performs a partial migration. As soon as the business of incubation is over, and the young are sufficiently grown to provide for themselves, he leaves his retirement,† and again draws near the habitations of mankind: his well-known familiarity has attracted the at-

* Unum arbustum non alit duos erithacos.

† The Redbreast, as well as some other kinds of birds, visits the sea-shores in the autumn.

tention and secured the protection of man in all ages ;
he haunts the dwelling of the cottager, and partakes of
his humble fare : when the cold grows severe, and snow
covers the ground, he approaches the house, taps at the
window with his bill, as if to entreat an asylum, which
is always chearfully granted, and with a simplicity the
most delightful, hops round the house, picks up crumbs,
and seems to make himself one of the family. Thomson has described the annual visits of this little guest,
in the following lines :—

> " The Redbreast, sacred to the household gods,
> " Wisely regardful of th' embroiling sky,
> " In joyless fields and thorny thickets leaves
> " His shivering mates, and pays to trusted man
> " His annual visit. Half afraid, he first
> " Against the window beats ; then brisk alights
> " On the warm hearth ; then, hopping o'er the floor,
> " Eyes all the smiling family askance,
> " And pecks, and starts, and wonders where he is ;
> " Till, more familiar grown, the table crumbs
> " Attract his slender feet."

The young Redbreast, when full feathered, may be
taken for a different bird, being all over besprinkled
with rust-coloured spots on a light ground : the first
appearance of the red is about the end of August, but
it does not attain its full colour till the end of the following month. Redbreasts are never seen in flocks,
but always singly ; and, when all other birds associate
together, they still retain their solitary habits. Buffon
says, that as soon as the young birds have attained their
full plumage, they prepare for their departure ; but in
thus changing their situation, they do not gather in

flocks, but perform their journey singly, one after another, which is a singular circumstance in the history of this bird. Its general familiarity has occasioned it to be distinguished by a peculiar name in many countries: about Bornholm, it is called Tomi Liden; in Norway, Peter Ronsmad; in Germany, it is called Thomas Gierdet; and with us, Robin-Redbreast, or Ruddock.

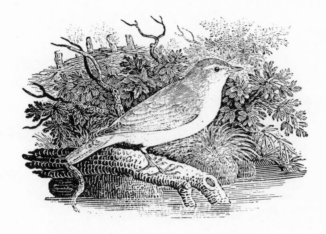

THE PASSERINE WARBLER.

(Motacilla passerina, Linn.—*La Passerinette,* Buff.)

LENGTH nearly the same as the last. Bill pale brown; upper parts of the body brown, tinged with olive green ; under parts dingy white, a little inclining to brown across the breast; quills dusky, with pale edges; tail dusky; over each eye is an indistinct whitish line : legs pale brown. The male and female are said to be much alike. The eggs are dull white irregularly marked with dusky spots. This bird is also a mocker, but its song is not so powerful as that of the last. Our specimen is somewhat less, and of a paler plumage than the Garden Warbler, but whether it may be the female, a variety, or a distinct species, the author has never been able to ascertain.

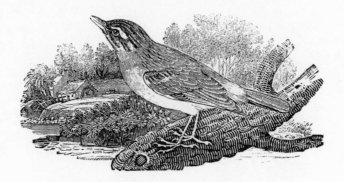

THE REED WARBLER.

SEDGE BIRD, OR REED WREN.

(Motacilla Salicaria, Linn.—*La Fauvette de roseaux,*
Buff.)

LENGTH five inches. Bill dusky; eyes hazel; crown
of the head and back brown, with dusky streaks; rump
tawny; cheeks brown; over each eye a light streak;
wing coverts dusky, edged with pale brown, as are the
quills and tail; throat, breast, and belly are white, the
latter tinged with yellow; thighs yellow; legs dusky;
the hinder claws much bent.

It frequents the sides of rivers and ponds, and also
places where reeds and sedges grow, and builds there;
the nest is made of dried grass, and tender fibres of
plants, lined with hair, and usually contains five eggs
of a dirty white, mottled with brown: it sings night and
day, during the breeding time, imitating by turns the
notes of various birds, from which it is also called the
English Mock bird. The whole of this genus are so shy,
that they will quit the nest if it be touched by any one.

THE BLACK-CAP

(Motacilla Atricapilla, Linn.—*La Fauvette à tête noire,*
Buff.*)*

Is somewhat above five inches in length. The upper mandible is of a dark horn colour; the under one
light blue, and the edges of both whitish; top of the
head black; sides of the head and hinder part of the
neck ash colour; back and wings olive grey; the throat,
breast, belly, and vent more or less silvery white; the
legs bluish, inclining to brown; claws black. The
head of the female is of a dull rust colour.

The Black-cap visits us about the middle of April,
and retires in September; it frequents gardens, and
builds its nest near the ground, commonly among the
branches of the woodbine; it is very slightly made, and
composed of the dried stems and curled roots of small
grass, thinly interwoven with a very few hairs, and
bound to the twigs with the cotton of plants; the inside
of the nest is deep and round; the eggs, commonly five
in number, are reddish brown, sprinkled or marbled

with spots of a much darker colour. During the time of incubation the male sits by turns, he likewise procures the female food, such as flies, worms, and insects. The Black-cap sings sweetly, and so like the Nightingale, that in Norfolk it is called the Mock-Nightingale; it also imitates the Thrush and the Blackbird. Our ingenious countryman, White, observes, that it has usually a full, sweet, deep, loud, and wild pipe, yet the strain is of short continuance, and its motions desultory; but when this bird sits calmly, and in earnest engages in song, it pours forth very sweet but inward melody, and expresses great variety of sweet and gentle modulations, superior, perhaps, to any of our warblers, the Nightingale excepted; and, while it warbles, its throat is wonderfully distended. Blackcaps feed chiefly on flies and insects, but not unfrequently on ivy and other berries, and the seeds of the evonymus.

THE YELLOW WREN,

WOOD WREN.

(Motacilla trochilus, Linn.—*Le Pouillot ou le Chantre,*
Buff.)

LENGTH above five inches. The bill is brown, the
inside and edges yellow; eyes hazel; upper parts of the
plumage yellow, inclining to a pale olive green; the
under pale yellow; over each eye there is a whitish
streak, which in young birds is very distinct; the
wings and tail are dusky brown, with pale edges: legs
yellowish brown.

There are three distinct species* of these, of which

---

* The Author was so fortunate as to procure specimens of each
kind, taken at the same time of the year, and had an opportunity of
noticing the difference of their song. For these specimens, as well

the Yellow Wren is the largest; the following two
differ in their size as well as note; their form and manners are, however, very similar. This species is rather
scarce here. It is sometimes seen on the tops of trees,
whence it often rises singing; its note is rather low,
and soft, but not much varied. It builds its nest in
plantations or coppices, and on the ground; it is composed of a great quantity of materials which lie scattered about, such as the leaves of the holly, which have
been dissected by insects, for its covering, and lined
with the withered stems of small grasses: the entrance
is on the side. The eggs, about six in number, are
white, and more or less closely spotted with deep
brown.

as for many others, this work is indebted to the late Major H. F.
Gibson, of the 4th dragoons.

A nest, of this species, with five young ones, was found and examined in Axwell Park, June 18, 1801: it was built in a hole on
the edge of a *brae*: the entrance was long, and curiously arched over
with the stems of dried grass.

THE WREN.

KITTY WREN.

(Motacilla Troglodytes, Linn.—*Le Troglodyte*, Buff.)

LENGTH three inches and a half. The bill is slender, and a little curved; upper mandible and tips of a brownish horn colour, the under one, and edges of both, dull yellow; a whitish line extends from the bill over the eyes, which are dark hazel; the upper parts of the plumage are clear brown, obscurely marked on the back and rump with narrow double wavy lines of pale and dark brown colours; the belly, sides, and thighs are marked with the same colours, but more distinctly; the throat is dingy white; cheeks and breast the same, faintly dappled with brown; the quills and tail are marked with alternate bars of a reddish brown and black; legs pale olive brown.

This active little bird is very common in England, and braves our severest winters, which it contributes

to enliven by its sprightly note. During that season
it approaches near the dwellings of man, and takes
shelter in the roofs of houses, barns, and in hay-stacks;
it sings till late in the evening, and not unfrequently
during a fall of snow. In the spring it betakes itself
to the woods, where it builds on the ground, or in a
low bush, and sometimes on the turf, beneath the
trunk of a tree, or in a hole in a wall: its nest is constructed with much art, of an oval shape, with one
small aperture in the side for an entrance: it is composed chiefly of moss, or other surrounding materials,
so as not to be easily distinguished from them, and
lined within with feathers: the female lays from ten to
sixteen, and sometimes eighteen eggs; they are white,
thinly sprinkled with small reddish spots, mostly at the
thicker end.

THE CRESTED TITMOUSE.

(Parus cristatus, Linn.*—Le Mésange Huppée.)*

THIS shy and solitary species is rather more than
four inches and a half in length. It is distinguished
from the rest of the genus by having its head ornamented with a peaked crest of black feathers, narrowly margined with white; those between the crest and the brow
are of the same colours, but the white greatly predominates. The bill and irides are dusky; the cheeks,
and sides of the head and neck dull white; the chin,
and fore part of the neck to the breast black; from
thence a line of the same branches off, and bounding
the white part of the neck, extends to the hinder part
of the head; the auriculars, with the exception of a
white spot in the middle, are black, and form a patch,
which is pointed off towards the nape; the back and

coverts are rusty dull brown; the quills and tail nearly
the same, but more deeply tinged with rust colour; the
breast, belly, and sides also partake of the same colours,
but are much paler; the legs are lead colour, tinged
with pale brown.

Some of the species have been met with in Scotland,
but are considered rare visitants. They take up their
abode in the deep recesses of forests, in various parts
of the continent of Europe, and prefer the shelter of
evergreen trees; but from their being of so retired a
disposition, they are seldom seen there, even by the
few whose business may lead them into these gloomy
wilds. The above figure was made from a preserved
specimen obligingly lent to this work by the Hon. H.
T. Liddell, of Ravensworth Castle.

THE MARSH TITMOUSE.

BLACK-CAPPED TITMOUSE.

(Parus palustris, Linn.—*La Mésange de marais,* Buff.)

LENGTH somewhat short of five inches. Bill black; the whole crown of the head, and part of the neck behind, deep black; a broad streak, of a yellowish white, passes from the beak, underneath the eye, backwards; throat black; breast, belly, and sides dirty white; back ash grey; quill feathers dusky, with pale edges: tail dusky; legs dark lead grey.

The Marsh Titmouse is said to be fond of wasps, bees, and other insects, and to lay up a little store of seeds against a season of want. It frequents marshy places, whence it derives its name. Its manners are similar to those of the Coal Titmouse, and it is equally prolific.

THE COCK.

(Phasianus Gallus, Linn.—*Le Coq*, Buff.)

THE Cock, like the Dog, in his present state of domestication, differs so widely from his supposed wild
original, as to render it a difficult matter to trace him
back to his primitive stock; however it is generally
agreed that he is to be found in a state of nature in the
forests of India, and in most of the islands of the Indian seas. The varieties of this species are endless,
every country and almost every district of each country,

producing a different kind.   From Asia, where they are supposed to have originated, they have been diffused over every part of the inhabited world.   America was the last to receive them.   It has been said that they were first introduced into Brazil by the Portuguese: they are now as common in all the inhabited parts of that vast continent as with us.   Of those which have been selected for domestic purposes in this country, the principal are—

1. The Crested Cock, of which there are several varieties, such as the white-crested black ones; the black-crested white ones; the gold and silver ones, &c.

2. The Hamburgh Cock, named also Velvet Breeches, because its thighs and belly are of a soft black.* This is a very large kind, and much used for the table.

3. The Bantam, or Dwarf Cock, a diminutive but very spirited breed: its legs are furnished with long feathers, which reach to the ground behind; it is very courageous, and will fight with one much stronger than itself.

4. The Frizzled Cock.   The feathers in this are so curled up that they seem to be reversed, and to stand in opposite directions.   They are originally from the southern parts of Asia, and when young are extremely sensible of cold.   They have a disordered and unpleasant appearance, but are in much esteem for the table.

5. The Silk Fowls, whose skin and bones are black.

6. A kind which has no rump, and consequently no tail feathers.

We shall finish our list with the English Game-Cock,

* Buffon.

which stands unrivalled by those of any other country
for its invincible courage, and on that account is made
use of as the instrument of the cruel diversion of cock-
fighting.   To trace this custom to its origin we must
look back into ancient times.   The Athenians allot-
ted one day in the year to cock-fighting; the Romans
are said to have learned it from them; and by that
warlike people it was first introduced into this island.
Henry VIII. was so attached to the sport, that in order to enjoy it, he caused a commodious house to be
erected, which, though it is now applied to a very different purpose, still retains the name of the Cock-pit.
The Chinese and many of the nations of India are so
extravagantly fond of this unmanly and disgraceful a-
musement, that, during the paroxysms of their phrensy,
they will sometimes risk not only the whole of their
property, but their wives and children, on the issue of
a battle.

The appearance of the Game-cock, when in his full
plumage and not mutilated for the purpose of fighting,
is strikingly beautiful and animated: his head, which
is small, is adorned with a beautiful red comb, and his
chin and throat with wattles; his eyes sparkle with
fire, and his whole demeanor bespeaks boldness and
freedom.   The feathers on his neck are long, slender,
and pointed, and fall gracefully down upon his body,
which is thick, muscular, and compact; his tail is
long, and the flexile feathers which fall over it form a
beautiful arch behind, which gives a grace to all his
motions: his legs are strong, and armed with sharp
spurs, with which he defends himself and attacks his
adversary; he lays hold with his beak, and strikes with

the feet and wings. When surrounded by his females, his whole aspect is full of animation; he allows of no competitor, but on the approach of a rival, rushes forward to instant combat, and either drives him from the field, or perishes in the attempt. He is polygamous, but this is a habit probably forced upon him by domestication, for even in this state, there is always one female more favoured than the rest, yet he is very attentive to his seraglio, hardly ever losing sight of them; he leads, defends, and cherishes them, collects them together when they straggle, and seems to eat unwillingly till he sees them feeding around him: when he loses them he utters his griefs aloud, and from the different inflections of his voice, and the various significant gestures which he makes, one would be led to conclude that it is a species of language which serves to communicate his sentiments. The fecundity of the hen is great; she lays generally two eggs in three days, and continues to lay through the greater part of the year, excepting the time of moulting, which lasts about two months. After having laid about ten or twelve eggs, she prepares for the anxious task of incubation, and gives the most certain indications of her wants by her cries, cluckings, and the violence of her emotions. Should she be deprived of her own eggs, she will cover those of any other kind, or even fictitious ones of stone or chalk, by which means she wastes herself in fruitless efforts. A sitting hen is a lively emblem of the most affectionate solicitude; she covers her eggs with her wings and body, fosters them with a genial warmth, and changes them gently, that all parts may be properly heated: she seems to perceive the impor-

tance of her employment, on which she is so intent,
that she apparently neglects, in some measure, the
necessary supplies of food and drink; she omits no
care, overlooks no precaution, to complete the existence of the little incipient beings, and to guard against
the dangers that threaten them; the cock takes upon
himself no part of the duty. Buffon, with his usual
elegance, observes, " that the condition of a sitting
hen, however insipid it may appear to us, is perhaps
not a tedious situation, but a state of continual joy; so
much has nature connected raptures with whatever relates to the multiplication of her creatures !"

When once the young have escaped from the shell,
her whole nature appears to undergo a transformation.
From being the most insensible and timid of birds, she
becomes impatient, anxious, and fearless, attacking
every animal, however fierce or powerful, that but
seems to threaten her tender brood.

For a curious account of the process of incubation,
in the developement of the chick, we refer our readers
to the above-mentioned author, who has given a minute
detail of the several appearances, till the chick is ready
to come forth.

The Egyptians have a method of hatching eggs without the assistance of the hen, and in great numbers at
once, by means of artificial heat. A similar practice
has been introduced into this country. The process is
managed by steam, and patents taken out for it !

THE PHEASANT.

(Phasianus Colchicus, Linn.—*Le Faisan,* Buff.)

LENGTH two feet eleven inches. The bill is of a pale
horn colour; the nostrils are hid under an arched covering; eyes yellow, and surrounded by a space in
appearance like scarlet cloth, finely spotted with black;
immediately under each eye is a small patch of short
feathers of a dark glossy purple; the upper parts of
the head and neck are deep purple, varying to glossy

green and blue; lower parts of the neck and the breast reddish chesnut, with black indented edges; the sides and lower part of the breast the same, with pretty large tips of black to each feather, which in different lights vary to a glossy purple; the belly and vent are dusky; back and scapulars beautifully variegated with black and white, or cream colour speckled with black, and mixed with deep orange, all the feathers edged with black; on the lower part of the back is a mixture of green; the quills are dusky, freckled with white; wing coverts brown, glossed with green, and edged with white; rump plain reddish brown; the two middle feathers of the tail are about twenty inches long, the shortest on each side less than five, of a reddish brown, marked with transverse bars of black: legs dusky, with a short blunt spur on each, but in some old birds the spurs are as sharp as needles; between the toes there is a strong membrane.

The female is less, and does not exhibit that variety and brilliancy of plumage which distinguish the male: the general colours are light and dark brown, mixed with black, the breast and belly finely freckled with small black spots on a light ground; the tail is short, and barred somewhat like that of the male; the space round the eye is covered with feathers.*

* The hen Pheasant is sometimes known, when she has done breeding, to assume the garb of a male. That illustrious physiologist, John Hunter, in a paper read before the Royal Society, and published in the Philosophical Transactions for 1780, says—" It is remarked by those who are conversant with this bird, when wild, that there appears now and then a hen Pheasant with the feathers of the cock; and all that they have decided on this subject is, that this ani-

The Ring Pheasant is a fine variety of this species : its principal difference consists in a white ring, which encircles the lower part of the neck ; the colours of the plumage in general are likewise more distinct and vivid. A fine specimen of this bird was sent us by the Rev. William Turner, of Newcastle, from which the figure was engraven. They are sometimes met with in the neighbourhood of Alnwick, whither they were brought by his Grace the late Duke of Northumberland. That they intermix with the common breed is very obvious, as in some we have seen, the ring was hardly visible, and in others a few feathers only, marked with white, appeared on each side of the neck, forming a white spot. It is much to be regretted, that this beautiful breed is likely soon to be destroyed, by those who pursue every species of game with an avaricious and indiscriminating rapacity.

There are many varieties of Pheasants, of extraordinary beauty and brilliancy of colours : in many gentlemen's woods there is a kind as white as snow, which will intermix with the common ones. Many of the gold and silver kinds, brought from China, are also kept in aviaries in this kingdom : the Common Phea-

mal does not breed, and that its spurs do not grow." He further notices, that in two of these birds which he dissected, he found them perfectly feminine, having " both the ovaria and the ovi-duct." A Pheasant exhibiting the same kind of plumage as those mentioned by Mr Hunter, was shot in January, 1805, by Sir Thomas Frankland, Bart. and presented to this work. This bird was of the size of the common hen Pheasant, its tail nearly the same ; it was without spurs, and had no scarlet around the eyes, and in rising its cry was that of the hen : in other respects its plumage was nearly like that of the male, only not quite so brilliant in colour.

sant is likewise a native of the east, and is the only one
of its kind that has multiplied in our island. Pheasants are generally found in low woody places, on the
borders of plains, where they delight to sport : during
the night they roost on the branches of trees. They
are very shy birds, and do not associate together, except during the months of March and April, when the
male seeks the female; they are then easily discoverable by the noise which they make in crowing and clap-
ping their wings, which may be heard at some distance.
The hen makes her nest on the ground, like the Partridge, and lays from twelve to fifteen olive coloured
eggs, which are smaller than those of the domestic
Hen : the young follow the mother as soon as they are
freed from the shell. During the breeding season the
cock Pheasants will sometimes intermix with our common Hen, and produce a hybrid breed, of which we
have known several instances.

THE PEACOCK.

(Pavo cristatus, Linn.—*Le Paon,* Buff.)

To describe the inimitable beauties of this bird, in
adequate terms, would be a task of no small difficulty.
" Its matchless plumage," says Buffon, " seems to
combine all that delights the eye in the soft and de-

licate tints of the finest flowers, all that dazzles it in the sparkling lustre of the gems, and all that astonishes it in the grand display of the rainbow." Its head is a-dorned with a tuft, consisting of twenty-four feathers, whose slender shafts are furnished with webs only at the ends, painted with the most exquisite green, mixed with gold : the head, throat, neck, and breast, are of a deep blue glossed with green and gold ; the back of the same, tinged with bronze ; the scapulars and lesser wing coverts reddish cream colour, variegated with black ; the middle coverts deep blue, glossed with green and gold ; the greater coverts and bastard wing reddish brown, as are also the quills, some of which are varie-gated with black and green ; the belly and vent are black, with a greenish hue ; but the distinguishing cha-racter of this singular bird is its train, which rises above the tail, and, when erected, forms a fan of the most re-splendent hues : the two middle feathers are sometimes four feet and a half long, the others gradually diminish-ing on each side ; the shafts, which are white, are fur-nished from their origin nearly to the end, with parted filaments of varying colours ending in a flat vane, which is decorated with what is called *the eye*. " This is a brilliant spot, enamelled with the most enchanting co-lours ; yellow, gilded with various shades ; green, run-ning into blue and bright violet, varying according to its different positions ; the whole receiving additional lustre from the colour of the centre, which is a fine velvet black." When pleased or delighted, and in the sight of his females, the Peacock erects his train, and displays the majesty of his beauty : all his movements are full of dignity ; his head and neck bend nobly back ;

his pace is slow and solemn, and he frequently turns
slowly and gracefully round, as if to catch the sun-
beams in every direction and produce new colours of
inconceivable richness, accompanied at the same time
with a hollow murmuring voice.   The cry of the Peacock, at other times, especially on a summer evening
and night, is often repeated, and is very disagreeable.

The Peahen is somewhat less than the cock, and
though furnished both with a train and crest, is destitute of those dazzling beauties by which he is distinguished. She lays five or six whitish eggs, in some
secret spot, where she can conceal them from the male,
who is apt to break them : she sits from twenty-five to
thirty days, according to the temperature of the climate
or season.

These birds were originally brought from the distant
parts of India, and thence have been diffused over the
civilized world.   The first notice of them is to be found
in holy writ,* where we are told they made part of the
cargoes of the valuable fleet which every three years
imported the treasures of the East to Solomon's court.
They are sometimes found wild in many parts of Asia
and Africa: the largest and finest are said to be met
with in the neighbourhood of the Ganges, and on the
fertile plains of India, where they attain a great size :
under the influence of that climate this beautiful bird
exhibits its dazzling colours, which seem to vie with the
gems and precious stones produced in those delightful
regions.   In colder climates they require great care in
rearing, and do not obtain their full plumage till the

* 2d Chron. ix. 21.

third year. Though rarely brought to the table now,
they were in former times considered a delicacy, and
made a part of the luxurious entertainments of the Roman voluptuaries.

The females sometimes assume the plumage of the
male; this is said to take place after they have done
laying. A bird of this kind is preserved in the British
Museum.

White Peacocks are not uncommon in England; the
eyes of the train are barely visible, and may be traced
by a different undulation of shade upon the pure white
of the tail.

THE PARTRIDGE.

(Tetrao Perdix, Linn.—*La Perdrix Grise,* Buff.)

LENGTH about thirteen inches. Bill light brown :
eyes hazel ; the general colour of its plumage is brown
and ash, beautifully mixed with black ; each feather
streaked down the middle with buff; the sides of the
head are tawny ; under each eye is a small saffron-co-
loured spot, which has a granulated appearance, and
between the eye and the ear a naked skin of a bright
scarlet, which is not very conspicuous but in old birds ;
on the breast there is a crescent of a deep chesnut ; the
tail is short and drooping : the legs are greenish white,
and furnished with a small knob behind. The female
has no crescent on the breast, and her colours in general are not so distinct and bright as those of the male.
The moult takes place once a year.

Partridges are found chiefly in temperate climates ;
the extremes of heat and cold being equally unfavour-
able to them : they are no where in greater plenty than

in this island, where, in their season, they contribute to our entertainments. It is much to be regretted, however, that the means taken to preserve this valuable bird should in a variety of instances, prove its destruction : the proper guardians of the eggs and young ones, tied down by ungenerous restrictions, are led to consider them as a growing evil, and not only connive at their destruction, but too frequently assist in it.

Partridges pair early in the spring, and once united it is rare that any thing but death separates them : the female lays from fourteen to eighteen or twenty eggs, making her nest of dry leaves and grass upon the ground. The young birds run as soon as hatched, frequently encumbered with part of the shell. It is no unsual thing to introduce Partridge's eggs under the Common Hen, who hatches and rears them as her own : in this case the young birds require to be fed with ants' eggs, which are their favourite food, and without which it is almost impossible to bring them up; they likewise eat insects, and when full grown, all kinds of grain and young plants. The affection of the Partridge for her young is peculiarly strong and lively; she is greatly assisted in the care of rearing them by her mate: they lead them out in common, call them together, gather for them their proper food, and assist in finding it by scratching the ground; they frequently sit close by each other, covering the chickens with their wings, like the Hen. In this situation they are not easily flushed; the sportsman, who is attentive to the preservation of his game, will carefully avoid giving any disturbance to a scene so truly interesting; but should the pointer come too near, or unfortunately run in upon

them, there are few who are ignorant of the confusion
that follows : the male first gives the signal of alarm by
a peculiar cry of distress, throwing himself at the same
moment more immediately in the way of danger, in order to deceive or mislead the enemy ; he flies, or rather
runs, along the ground, hanging his wings, and exhibiting every symptom of debility, whereby the dog is
decoyed, in the too eager expectation of an easy prey,
to a distance from the covey; the female flies off in a
contrary direction, and to a greater distance, but returning soon after by secret ways, she finds her scattered brood closely squatted among the grass, and collecting them with haste, leads them from the danger,
before the dog has had time to return from his pursuit.

THE QUAIL.

(Tetrao Coturnix, Linn.—*La Caille,* Buff.)

LENGTH seven inches and a half. Bill dusky; eyes
hazel; the colours of the head, neck, and back are a
mixture of brown, ash, and black; over each eye there
is a yellowish streak, extending behind the auriculars,
and another of the same over the middle of the forehead to the nape; a dark lines passes from each corner
of the bill, forming a kind of divided gorget about the
throat; the scapular feathers are marked by a light
yellowish streak down the middle of each; quills
lightish brown, with small rust-coloured bands on the
exterior edges of the feathers; the breast is pale rusty,
spotted with black, and streaked with pale yellow; the
tail consists of twelve feathers, barred like the wings;
belly and thighs yellowish white: legs pale brown.
The female wants the black spots on the breast, and is
easily distinguished by a less vivid plumage.

Quails are very generally diffused throughout Asia,
Africa, and the southern parts of Europe, but rare in

temperate climates; they are birds of passage, and are seen in immense flocks flying across the Mediterranean, from Europe to the shores of Africa, in the autumn, and returning again in the spring, frequently alighting in their passage on the intervening islands, particularly of the Archipelago, which they almost cover with their numbers. On the western coasts of the kingdom of Naples such prodigious numbers have appeared, than an hundred thousand have been taken in a day within the space of four or five miles. From these circumstances it appears highly probable, that the Quails which supplied the Israelites with food, during their journey through the wilderness, were driven thither on their passage to the north, by a wind from the south-west, sweeping over Ethiopia and Egypt towards the shores of the Red Sea. Quails are not very numerous here; they breed with us, and many of them are said to remain throughout the year, changing their quarters from the interior to the sea coast. The female makes her nest like the Partridge, and lays to the number of six or seven* eggs of a greyish colour, speckled with brown. The young birds follow the mother as soon as hatched, but do not continue long together; they are scarcely grown up before they separate; or, if kept together, they fight obstinately, their quarrels frequently terminating in each other's destruction. From this quarrelsome disposition in the

* In France they are said to lay fifteen or twenty. *Buff.*

They are sometimes seen in a bevy of fifteen together, in this country; and while running through the meadows, are known by their quickly repeated short whistle of " whit, whit." They fly quick and near the ground.

Quail they were made use of by the Greeks and Romans as we use Game-cocks, for the purpose of fighting. We are told that Augustus punished a prefect of Egypt with death, for bringing to his table one of these birds, which had acquired celebrity by its victories. The Chinese are much addicted to the amusement of fighting Quails, and in some parts of Italy it is said likewise to be no unusual practice. After feeding two Quails very highly, they place them opposite, and throw in a few grains of seeds between them; the birds rush upon each other with the utmost fury, striking with their bills and heels till one of them yields.

THE GREAT BUSTARD.*

(Otis Tarda, Linn.—*L'Outarde,* Buff.)

THIS very singular bird, which is the largest of our
land birds, is about four feet long, and weighs from
twenty-five to thirty pounds; its characters are peculi-

---

* Drawn from a preserved specimen at Wycliffe.

ar, and with such as connect it with birds of the galli-
naceous kind, it has others which seem to belong to the
Ostrich and the Cassowary. The bill is strong, and
rather convex; the eyes red; on each side of the root
of the lower mandible there is a tuft of feathers about
nine inches long; the head and neck are ash coloured.
In the one described by Edwards, there were on each
side of the neck two naked spots, of a violet colour,
but which appeared to be covered with feathers when
the neck was much extended. The back is barred
transversely with black and bright rusty on a pale reddish ground; the quills are black; belly white: the
tail consists of twenty feathers; the middle ones are
rufous, barred with black; those on each side are
white, with a bar or two of black near the ends: the
legs are long, naked above the knees, and dusky; it
has no hind toe; the nails are short, strong, and convex both above and below; the bottom of the foot is
furnished with a callous prominence, which serves instead of a heel. The female is not much more than
half the size of the male: the top of her head is deep
orange, the rest of the head brown; her colours are
not so bright as those of the male, and she has no tuft
on each side of the head. There is likewise another
very essential difference between the male and the female: the former is furnished with a sack or pouch,[*]
situated in the fore part of the neck, and capable of
containing about two quarts; the entrance to it is immediately under the tongue.[†] This singular reservoir

* Temminck does not notice this pouch.
† Barrington's Misc. p. 553.

was first discovered by Dr Douglas, who supposes that the bird fills it with water as a supply in the midst of those dreary plains where it is accustomed to wander;* it likewise makes a further use of it in defending itself against the attacks of birds of prey; on such occasions it throws out the water with such violence as to baffle the pursuit of its enemy.

Bustards were formerly more common in this island than at present; they are now found only in the open countries of the South and East, in the plains of Wiltshire, Dorsetshire, and in some parts of Yorkshire; they were formerly met with in Scotland, but are now extinct there. They are slow in taking wing, but run with great rapidity, and when young are sometimes taken with greyhounds, which pursue them with great avidity: the chace is said to afford excellent diversion. The Great Bustard is granivorous, but feeds also on herbs of various kinds; it is likewise fond of those worms which come out of the ground in great numbers before sun-rise in the summer; in winter it frequently feeds on the bark of trees: like the Ostrich, it swallows small stones,† bits of metal, and the like. The female builds no nest, but making a hole on the ground, drops two eggs, about the size of those of a Goose, of a pale olive brown, with dark spots. She

---

* One of these birds, which was kept in a caravan, among other animals, as a show, lived without drinking. It was fed with leaves of cabbages and other greens, and also with flesh and bread.

† In the stomach of one which was opened by the academicians, there were found, besides small stones, to the number of ninety doubloons, all worn and polished by the attrition of the stomach. —*Buff.*

sometimes leaves her eggs in quest of food; and if, during her absence, any one should handle, or even breathe
upon them, she immediately abandons them.

Bustards are found in various parts of Europe, Asia,
and Africa, but have not hitherto been discovered in
the new continent.

THE GREAT PLOVER.*

THICK-KNEE'D BUSTARD, STONE CURLEW, NORFOLK
PLOVER.

(Charadrius Oedicnemus, Linn.—*Le grand Pluvier,*
Buff.)

LENGTH about sixteen inches. The bill is long, yellowish at the base, and black at the tip; irides and orbits pale yellow; above each eye there is a pale streak,
and beneath one of the same colour extends to the bill;

* Montagu makes this a Bustard—the bill and webbed roots of the
toes would hardly allow this arrangement; it is evidently more allied
to the Plover. The distance of the base of the bill from the eye, and
likewise its food and habits are different from the former.

throat white; head, neck, and all the upper parts of the body pale tawny brown; down the middle of each feather there is a dark streak; fore part of the neck and the breast nearly of the same colour, but much paler; belly, thighs, and vent pale yellowish white; quills black; tail short and rounded, and a dark band crosses the middle of each feather; the tips black, the rest white: legs yellow, and naked above the knees, which are very thick, as if swollen, hence its name; claws black.

This bird is found in great plenty in Norfolk and several of the southern counties, but is no where to be met with in the northern parts of our island; it prefers dry and stony places, on the sides of sloping banks. It makes no nest: the female lays two or three eggs on the bare ground, sheltered by a stone, or in a small hole formed in the sand; they are of a dirty white, marked with spots of a deep reddish colour, mixed with slight streaks. Although this bird has great power of wing, and flies with great strength, it is seldom seen during the day, except surprised, when it springs to some distance, and generally escapes before the sportsman comes within gun-shot; it likewise runs on the ground almost as swiftly as a dog; after running some time it stops short, holding its head and body still, and on the least noise, squats close on the ground. In the evening it comes out in quest of food, and may then be heard at a great distance: its cry is singular, resembling a hoarse kind of whistle three or four times repeated, and has been compared to the turning of a rusty handle. Buffon endeavours to express it by the words *turrlui, turrlui,* and says it resembles the sound

of a third flute, dwelling on three or four tones from a
flat to a sharp. Its food chiefly consists of worms. It
is said to be good eating when young; the flesh of the
old ones is hard, black, and dry. White mentions
them as frequenting the district of Selborne, in Hampshire. He says, that the young run immediately from
the nest, almost as soon as they are excluded, like Partridges; that the dam leads them to some stony field,
where they bask, skulking among the stones, which
they resemble so nearly in colour, as not easily to be
discovered.

Birds of this kind are migratory; they arrive in
April, live with us all the spring and summer, and at
the beginning of autumn prepare to take leave by get-
ting together in flocks: it is supposed that they retire
to Spain, and frequent the sheep-walks with which that
country abounds.

THE GOLDEN PLOVER.

YELLOW PLOVER.

(Charadrius Pluvialis, Linn.—*Le Pluvier doré,* Buff.)

LENGTH ten inches. Bill dusky; eyes dark; all the
upper parts of the plumage are marked with bright
yellow spots upon a dark brown ground; the fore part
of the neck and the breast are the same, but much
paler; the belly is almost white; the quills are dusky;
the tail is marked with dusky and yellow bars; the legs
are black. Birds of this species vary much from each
other; in some which we have had, the breast was
marked with black and white; in others, it was almost
black; but whether this difference arose from age or
sex, we are at a loss to determine.

The Golden Plover is common in this country and
all the northern parts of Europe; it is very numerous

in various parts of America, from Hudson's Bay as far as Carolina, migrating from one place to another, according to the seasons. It breeds on high and heathy mountains: the female lays four eggs, of a pale olive colour, variegated with blackish spots. They fly in small flocks, and make a shrill whistling noise, by an imitation of which they are sometimes enticed within gun-shot. The male and female do not differ from each other. In young birds the yellow spots are not very distinguishable, as the plumage inclines more to grey.

THE SANDERLING.

TOWILLEE, OR CURWILLET.

(Charadrius Calidris, Linn.—*Maubeche,* Buff.)

THIS bird weighs almost two ounces; is about eight
inches in length, and fifteen in breadth, from tip to tip.
The bill is an inch long, slender, black and grooved on
the sides nearly from the tip to the nostril; the brow
to the eyes white; rest of the head pale ash grey, mottled in brown streaks from the forehead to the hinder
part of the neck, and on each side of the upper part of
the breast; back, scapulars, and greater coverts, brownish ash, edged with dull white, and irregularly marked
with dark brown spots. The pinions, lesser coverts
and bastard wings, dark brown; the quills, which extend beyond the tail, are of the same colour on their
exterior webs and points, except four of the middle
ones, which are white on the outer webs, forming, when

the wing is closed, a sharp wedge-shaped spot; inner
webs brownish ash; secondary quills brown, tipped with
white; the rump and tail coverts also brown, edged
with dirty white; tail feathers brownish ash, edged with
a lighter shade, the two middle ones much darker than
the rest; throat, fore part of the neck, breast, belly,
thighs and vent white; the toes and legs black, and
bare a little above the knees. This bird is of a slender
form, and its plumage has a hoary appearance among
the Stints, with which it associates on the sea-shore, in
various parts of Great Britain. It wants the hinder
toe, and has, in other respects, the look of the Plover
and Dotterel, to which family it belongs.

Latham says, this bird, like the Purre, and some
others, varies considerably, either from age or the season; for those he received in August, had the upper
parts dark ash coloured, and the feathers deeply edged
with a ferruginous colour; but others sent him in January were of a plain dove-coloured grey; they differed also in some other trifling particulars.

A

HISTORY

OF

BRITISH BIRDS.

BY

THOMAS BEWICK.

VOL. II.

CONTAINING THE

HISTORY AND DESCRIPTION OF

WATER BIRDS.

NEWCASTLE:

PRINTED BY EDW. WALKER, PILGRIM-STREET,

FOR T. BEWICK: SOLD BY HIM, LONGMAN AND CO. LONDON;

AND ALL BOOKSELLERS.

1826.

THE PREFACE.

To point out the paths which lead to happiness, however remote they may lie from common observation, and at the same time to forewarn the inexperienced stranger against approaching those which terminate in vice and misery, is a task worthy of the most enlightened understanding. The learned in every age have laboured for these ends : they have set up their works like beacons and guide-posts, to direct their fellow travellers in the journey of life. These are their marks, left behind them to witness their having lived; and although, like other more vain human monuments, they remain but for a while—since, in the great scale of time, every work of man, like an inscription on the sea-sand, is washed away by the return of the ceaseless wave—yet let not this reflection, so mortifying to human vanity, damp the ardour of doing good ; for however temporary the efforts may be, they are not only valuable in themselves, (being records of usefulness laid up for the benefit of mankind) but are incitements also to the emulation of good example, whereby incalculable advantages may be derived to thousands yet unborn. he generality of men, indeed, are little affected by

observations of this sort : regardless of the voice of reason,
and lost to a sense of duty, they neither know nor enquire
why they were sent upon the stage of life ; they stumble on
still in darkness and error, and waste their days without a
single effort to be useful to the community in which they
live : they see not the wonders which the universe presents
to stimulate them to reflect on the wisdom, the power, and
the goodness, which planned and support the whole.   De-
spairing of their improvement, whose minds have thus been
suffered to grow up into maturity uncultivated, we should
rather direct our attention to the sowing of the seeds of
knowledge in the minds of youth.

The great work of forming the man cannot be begun too
early ; and, agreeably with this sentiment, how many writers
are there who spend their lives in contributing, in various
ways, to turn the streams of instruction through their proper
channels, into this most improveable soil ! Taking children
by the hand, from their leading-strings and go-carts, they
direct their steps, like guardian angels, in the outset of life,
to prevent their floundering on in ignorance to the end.   In
these undertakings the instructors of youth are often assisted by the fertile genius of the artist, who supplies their
works with such embellishments as serve to relieve the
lengthened sameness of the way. Among the many approved
branches of instruction, the study of Natural History holds
a distinguished rank. To enlarge upon the advantages which
are derivable from a knowledge of the creation, is surely not
necessary ; to become initiated into this knowledge, is to become enamoured of its charms ; to attain the object in view
requires but little previous study or labour ; the road which
leads to it soon becomes strewed with flowers, and ceases to
fatigue ; a flow is given to the imagination, which banishes
early prejudices and expands the ideas ; and an endless fund
of the most rational entertainment is spread out, which

captivates the attention and exalts the mind. For the attainment of this science, in any of its various departments, the foundation may be laid, insensibly, in youth, whereon this goodly superstructure of knowledge can easily be raised at a more advanced period. In whatever way, indeed, the varied objects of this beautiful world are viewed, they are readily understood by the contemplative mind, for they are found alike to be the visible words of God. " The Creator, doubtless, did not bestow so much curiosity and exquisite workmanship and skill upon his creatures, to be looked upon with a careless incurious eye."* Could mankind be prevailed upon to read a few lessons from the great book of Nature, so amply spread out before them, they would clearly see the hand of Providence in every page; and would they consider the faculty of reason as the distinguishing gift to the human race, and use it as the guide of their lives, they would find their reward in a cheerful resignation of mind, in peace and happiness, under the conscious persuasion, that a good naturalist cannot be a bad man.

In ideas congenial with these, originated the first incitements, which drew forth the Histories of Quadrupeds and British Birds. From these humble attempts—for every attempt to depicture nature must fall short of the original—it is hoped that some useful instruction may be gathered, and at the same time a stimulus excited to further enquiry. But however this may prove, " innocently to amuse the imagination in this dream of life, is wisdom ; and nothing is useless which, by furnishing mental employment, keeps us for a while in oblivion of those stronger appetites that lead to evil."† To the rising generation these efforts to instruct and please are principally directed, and are set forth with

* Derham's Physico-theology, Book xi. chap. 2.
† Goldsmith.

an ardent wish, that they may be found to deserve the notice
of youth, and contribute to amuse and to inform them. May
the reader, impressed with sentiments of humanity, on view-
ing the portraits, spare and protect the originals : and when
these books shall become obsolete, or be lost in the revolution of time, may some other more able naturalist arise
equally inclined to produce better to supply their place.

Thomas Bewick

Newcastle upon Tyne, December, 1805.

INTRODUCTION

TO THE

HISTORY OF BRITISH WATER BIRDS.

In the preceding volume of British Land Birds, the characters of that part of the first great division of the feathered
tribes, the beautiful tenants of the air, the woods, and the
fields, have been described, and their figures faithfully delineated.   Amongst these were enumerated not only the carnivorous and rapacious kinds, which by the accuracy of their
scent, discover putrid bodies at a vast distance, and those
which, endowed with piercing sight, soar aloft in search of
their living prey, and dart upon it from an immeasurable
height, with the rapidity of an arrow; but also the various
other kinds of land birds, which, although less noticed, are
eminently useful to man, by clearing the earth and the atmosphere of myriads of insects, in every stage of their progressive growth, from the invisible egg to the period when
they are enabled to flutter on the wing.   These, together

with the other branches of this great family, whose lives may
be said to be spent more innocently than those of the rapacious kinds, all contribute their services to man, by clearing
the earth of the seeds of noxious plants, as well as the trees
of innumerable destructive insects, with which they feed
their young, and claim for themselves, meanwhile, but a
small return of the produce of the fields and gardens, which
too often is ungratefully begrudged them.

Nearly the whole of this amusing group appear to relieve
each other, and are, in succession, the constant neighbours,
or attendants on the habitations of men. They are the sub-
tenants of the cultivated world, and most of them, especially
those that are granivorous, may well be termed wild poultry,
and are the valued property of the sportsman. Some of
these, also, uniting with others of the soft-billed tribe, form
the husbandman's cheerful band of choristers, whose comings
and goings proclaim the seasons ; while, by their notes, poured forth from every tree, and vale, and woody glen, they enliven the face of nature. But having described this division
of birds in the former volume, we must now bid them adieu,
with this testimony of their usefulness—that they are the in-
dustrious regulating little messengers of Providence, without
whose assistance the plough and the spade would often find
their labours bestowed in vain ; and weak as these instru-
ments may appear, without their aid, instead of a land of
overflowing plenty, adorned with flowers and fruits, and
trees and woods, in rich luxuriance, and in all their varied
beauty, where every grove is made vocal with responsive
praises, we should too frequently meet with nothing but the
barrenness, and the silence, and the dreariness of a desert.

Leaving those denizens* of nature to enjoy their own native woods, the sheltering coppice, or extended plain, the

* " Behold the fowls of the air, for they sow not, neither do they reap,
nor gather into barns, yet your heavenly father feedeth them."—See
Matt. vi. 26.

task now assigned us is to delineate the figures, and to describe the characters of the other two divisions of this numerous family—the *waders* and the *swimmers;* these are generally found far removed from the cultivated world. In exploring the tract which leads us, step by step, to an acquaintance with them, we must travel through reeds and rushes, with doubtful feet, over the moss-covered faithless quagmire, amidst oozing rills, and stagnant pools. The first division of these inhabitants of the marsh are called *waders.* All the genera, and the different species, of this division have divided toes : they are apparently fitted for living on land, but are furnished with propensities and appetites which direct them chiefly to seek their food in moist and watery places, or on the margins of lakes and rivers, and yet they avoid those depths, where it might seem to be found in the greatest abundance. Most of them have long bills, formed to perforate the soft mud and moist earth, and long legs, bare above the knees, whereby they are enabled to wade through shallow waters in search of food, without wetting their plumage. Others have shorter legs, feathered down to their knees, and bills of varied length : whence it may appear that these are more limited in their powers, and pick up only such insects or grasses, seeds or roots of aquatic plants, as are to be met with near the surface of the ground, or in shallow pools ; whilst others again are known to plunge into the water, and by partial swimmings to extricate themselves from it, after they have seized their prey, whether fishes or insects. Some of this class, in the warmer or temperate climates, breed and rear their young in the fens, where they remain throughout the year : others again, but these are few, after the business of incubation is over, disappear, and are supposed to direct their flight northward ; while others, and these by much the greater number, are known invariably to leave the north, and to migrate southward on the approach of the winter months, and to return northward in the spring. It must be observed that the swamps and inland waters of temperate climes, are also stocked with a numerous set of inhabitants of the second class—the *swimmers*. Some of these, likewise, after having reared their young, migrate much in the same way as the *waders*.

The ornithologist, who does not content himself with bare names and appearance, in examining the economy of the various kinds of birds, and the structure of their several parts, will find ample room for the exercise of his labours in the most minute investigation; and although he can scarcely overlook the slow, and almost imperceptible degrees, by which nature has removed one class of beings from another, yet in his attempts to trace the relationship, or affinity, which one bears to another, he will, with his utmost care, find himself at a loss to ascertain that precise link in the chain, where the doubtful crossing line is drawn, and by which the various genera and species are to be separated. But, however, after he shall have examined a few gradations, upwards or downwards, he will more readily discover the modes of life which the several kinds are destined to pursue; and their ability to perform the various evolutions necessary for the procuring of their food, in that exactitude to which the Author of Nature hath formed them. In some of those which run on the surface of the soft mud, and can occasionally take the water, the indications of their ability for swimming are furnished very sparingly : these indications first appear in the breadth of the under sides of the toes, with the two outer toes joined by a small web. The scalloped membranes attached to the sides of the toes form the next advance : some are webbed to the nails, with deep indentations in the middle, between each toe ; others have only three toes, all placed forwards, and fully united by webbed membranes : some have the addition of back toes, either plain, or with webbed appendages to each ; and others again have the four toes fully webbed together. The thighs, in the most expert divers, are placed very far back ; their legs are almost as flat and thin as a knife ; and they are enabled to fold up their toes so closely, that the least possible resistance is made while they are drawing them forward to repeat their strokes in the water. Many of these divers are provided internally with a receptacle, seated about the windpipe, for a stock of air, which serves the purpose of respiration, whilst they remain under water : and the whole of the tribe of swimmers have their feathers bedded upon a soft, close, warm down ; and are furnished with a natural oil, supplied from a gland in the rump. This oil they press out with their bills from a kind of nipple, and with it preen and dress their plumage, which is thereby rendered impenetrable to the water, and, in a great degree, to the most extreme cold.

Of the number of these birds, both waders and swimmers, a great proportion may not improperly be termed fresh-water birds, as they rear their young, and spend the greater part of their time inland. In this class are the *Ardea, Scolopax,* and *Tringa,* with divided toes—the *Fulica, Phalaropus,* and *Podiceps,* with finned feet ; together with others of the web-footed kinds, chiefly of the genera of the *Mergus* and *Anas.* Among these various kinds, some species are found, which only occasionally visit the sea-shore : others have not been noticed there at all ; while others are seen there frequently, feeding on the beach : some, like little boats, keep within bays and creeks, near the shores ; others, meanwhile, adventure into the ocean, and sport amidst its waves. To particularize these, with their various places of abode, and the times of their migrations, would here be tedious and unnecessary : they are noticed in the description of each bird.

The northern extremities of the earth seem as if they were set apart for the nations of the feathered race, as their pe-

culiar heritage—a possession which they have held coeval
with creation. There, amidst lakes and endless swamps,
where the human foot never trod, and where, excepting their
own cries, nothing is heard but the winds, they find an asylum
where they can rear their young in safety, unmolested, and
surrounded by a profusion of plenty. This ample provision
consists chiefly of the larvæ of gnats and other insects, with
which the atmosphere must be loaded in that region, during
the summer months. The eggs of these insects being deposited in the mud, and hatched by the influence of the unsetting summer's sun, they arise like exhalations, in multiplied
myriads, and, as we may conceive, afford a never-failing supply of food to the feathered tribes. An equal abundance of
food is also provided for the young of those kinds of birds
which seek it from the waters, in the spawn of fishes, or the
small fry, which fearlessly sport in their native element, undisturbed by the angler or the fisherman. In these retire-
ments they remain, or only change their haunts from one
lake or misty bog to another, to procure food, or to mix with
their kind; and thus they pass the long enlightened season.
As soon as the sun begins, in shortened peeps, to quit his
horizontal course, the falling snows, and the hollow blasts
foretel the change, and are the signals for their departure:
then it is, that the widely-spreading winged host, having gathered together, in separate tribes, their plump well-fledged
families, directed by instinctive knowledge, leave their native wilds, the arctic regions, that prolific source, whence
these multiplied migrators, in flocks innumerable, and in directions like radii from the centre of a circle, are poured
forth to replenish the more southern quarters of the globe.
In their route, they are impelled forwards, or stop short, in
greater or less numbers, according to the severity or mildness
of the season, and are thus more equally distributed over the
cultivated world; where man, habituated to consider every

thing in the creation as subservient to his use, and ever watchful to seize all within his grasp, makes them feel the full force of his power. Wherever they settle under his dominion, these pretty wanderers afford a supply to the wants of some, pamper the luxury of others, and keep the eager sportsman in constant employment.

Leaving the lakes and inland watery wastes, to pursue his researches by the brooks and the rivers, in their lengthened course to the estuaries and to the sea, the ornithologist is delighted with the view of the various clean-feathered inhabitants, feeding or preening themselves on the shores, swimming or diving in the current, or wheeling aloft on the wing, Many of these divide their time between the fresh and the salt waters, and serve as aerial guides, to direct his sight over the vast expanse, to other classes of birds that almost entirely commit themselves to the ocean; and with those tribes at certain seasons, these associate. This multifarious host, thus assembled in distinct families, is sometimes seen to cover the surface of the water to a vast extent : and of all these various families, those of the *Anas* genus, which keep much at sea, form the most considerable, amounting in the whole to ninety-eight species, besides varieties,* a number exceeding that of any other kind. And, when we consider that each family of this genus is often seen in considerable flocks, and add them to those which may more properly be called sea-fowl— beginning with the *Alca,* and ending with the *Pelecanus*— consisting of nine distinct British genera and their species, we shall find the aggregate far to exceed in number the whole of the birds that are supported on the land. Whilst these fishers, in their flying squadrons, are viewed from the

* It is very probable that many of these varieties, as well perhaps as others that are accounted distinct species, may be a mixed breed, the produce of a kind somewhat different; and that this may also be the case with the varieties of other genera of birds.

cliffs and shores of the sea, soaring aloft, or resting secure on the louring precipice, the ear is often pierced with their harsh shrill cries, screamed forth in mingled discord with the roaring of the surge. Grating as their cries are, these birds are often hailed by the mariner, as his only pilots, while he is tossed to and fro, amidst solitary rocks, and isles inhabited only by the sea fowl.

Although it is not certainly known to what places some of these kinds retire to breed, yet it is ascertained that the greater part of them hatch and rear their young on the rocky promontories and inlets of the sea, and on the innumerable little isles with which the extensive coast of Norway is studded, from its southern extremity—the Lindesness, or Naze, to the North Cape, that opposes itself to the Frozen Ocean. The Hebrides, or Western Scottish Isles, are also well known to be a principal rendezvous to sea-fowl, and celebrated as such by Thomson :—

" Or where the northern ocean, in vast whirls,
" Boils round the naked melancholy isles
" Of farthest *Thule;* and the Atlantic surge
" Pours in among the stormy *Hebrides:*
" Who can recount what transmigrations there
" Are annual made? What nations come and go?
" And how the living clouds on clouds arise?
" Infinite wings! till all the plume-dark air,
" And rude resounding shore are one wild cry."

Other parts of the world—the bleak shores and isles of Lapland, Siberia, Spitzbergen, Nova Zembla, Iceland, Greenland, &c. with the vast sweep of the Arctic Zone, are also enlivened in their seasons by swarms of sea-fowl, which range the intervening open parts of the seas to the shoreless frozen ocean. There a barrier is put to further enquiry, beyond which the prying eye of man must not look, and there his imagination only must take the view, to supply the place of reality. In these forlorn regions of *unknowable* dreary space, this reservoir of frost and snow, where firm fields of ice, the accumulations of centuries of winters, glazed in Alpine heights above heights, surround the pole, and concentre the multiplied rigours of extreme cold ; even here, so far as human intelligence has been able to penetrate, there appears to subsist an abundance of animals, in the air, and in the waters : and, perhaps, it may not be carrying conjecture too far to suppose that every region of the earth, air, and water, however ungenial the clime may appear to us, is replete with animals, suited, each kind, to the place assigned to it.

Certain it is, however, that the deeps of the frozen zone are the great receptacle whence the finny tribes issue, in so wonderful a profusion, to re-stock all the watery world of the northern hemisphere ; and that this immense icy protuberance of the globe, this gathering together, this hoard of congealed waters, is periodically diminished by the influence of the unsetting summer's sun, whose rays being perpetually, though obliquely, shed, during that season, on the widely extended rim of the frozen continent, gradually dissolve its margin, which is thus crumbled into innumerable floating isles, that are driven southward to replenish the seas of warmer climates.*

Amidst these drifts of ice, and following this widely spreading current, teeming with life, the whole host of sea-fowl find in the waters an inexhaustible supply of food : for the great movement, the immense southward migration of fishes is then begun, and shoal after shoal, probably as the removal of their dark icy canopy unveils them to the sun, are invited forth, and, guided by its light and heat, poured forward in thousands of myriads, in multitudes which set all calculation at defiance. The flocks of sea-birds, for their numbers, baffle

* The same happens in the southern hemisphere, by the melting of the ice at the south pole.

the power of figures ;* but the swarms of fishes, as if engen-
dered in the clouds, and showered down like the rain, are
multiplied in an incomprehensible degree : they may indeed
be called infinite, if infinity were applicable to any thing created. Of all these various tribes of fishes, thus pressing forward on their southern route, that of the Herring is the most
numerous. Closely embodied in resplendent columns of many
miles in length and breadth, and in depth from the surface
to the bottom of the sea, the shoals of this tribe peacefully
glide along, and glittering like a huge reflected rainbow, or
Aurora Borealis, attract the eyes of all their attendant foes.
Other kinds of fishes, in duller garbs, keep also together in
bodies, but change their movements as may best suit their
different modes of attack or defence, in preying upon, or
escaping from each other as they pass along.† All these various tribes of fishes, but particularly that of the Herring, are
in their turns encountered and preyed upon by the whole hosts
of sea-fowl, which continually watch all their motions. Some
are seen to hover over the shoals of fishes, and to wheel about
in quick and glancing evolutions, and then to dart down like

* A bird may lay ten eggs and hatch them; but the roe of a herring
is said to contain ten thousand.

† " Fishes are the most voracious animals in nature. Many species
prey indiscriminately on every thing digestible that comes in their way,
and devour not only other species of fishes, but even their own. As a
counterbalance to this voracity they are amazingly prolific. Some bring
forth their young alive ; others produce eggs. The viviparous *Blenny*
brings forth 200 or 300 live fishes at a time. Those which produce eggs
are all much more prolific, and seem to proportion their stock to the
danger of consumption. Lewenhock affirms that the Cod spawns above
nine millions in a season. The Flounder produces above one million,
and the Mackarel above 500,000. Scarcely one in a hundred of these
eggs, however, is supposed to come to maturity : but two wise purposes
are answered by this amazing increase; it preserves the species in the
midst of numberless enemies, and serves to furnish the rest with a sus-
tenance adapted to their nature."—*Encycl. Britan.*

a falling plummet upon the selected object, which is gliding near the surface of the water, and instantly to rise, and devour the living victim on the wing. Others, equally alert and rapid in their pursuit, plunge and dive after their prey to greater depths; while the less active birds seem content to devour only such of the fishes as have been killed or wounded, and cast out on the flanks, or left in the rear of the main body.

In this great, this wonderful migration of birds and fishes, it is evident that they are amply provided on their way with an abundance of food, which they derive from each other; and that the shoals of fishes which the sea-fowl attend, are impelled southward by instinct, aided by currents, for the accomplishment of their mission. The birds also, in their progress to fulfil the same high purpose, are by these enticed forward, as it were, to follow the seasons, and to wing their way to the posts assigned them in climes adapted to the fulfilling of the great duties of rearing their young, and of leading them forth to pursue the unalterable course of nature: and thus they spend out the varied year in the same ceaseless traversings on the globe.

Notwithstanding the prodigious multitudes of the inhabitants of the ocean, which are thus destroyed by each other, and by their winged enemies, yet, like a small toll, or like a measure of sand taken from the beach, there is no visible diminution of them; for although many divisions of the larger kinds, by keeping in the mid-sea deeps, escape notice, and are dispersed like the fowl that follow to feed on them; yet others are mixed with the smaller sorts, and form part of those vast shoals which yearly present themselves to man, filling every creek and inlet of the northern shores, particularly those of the British isles; where this wonderful influx appears as if offered to give employment to thousands, and to supply an inexhaustible source of commerce: but this, like other overflowing bounties of Providence, seems to be too little regarded : the waste, indeed, in this instance, is sufficient to feed half the human race,

It is a melancholy reflection, that, from man, downwards, to the smallest living creature, all are found to prey upon and devour each other. The philosophic mind, however, sees this waste of animal life again and again repaired by fresh stores, ever ready to supply the void, and the great work of generation and destruction perpetually going on, and to this dispensation of an all-wise Providence, so interesting to humanity, bows in awful silence.

In returning from these digressions to the subject of the present enquiry, let the imagination picture to itself countless multitudes of birds, wafted like the clouds, around the globe, which in ceaseless revolutions turns its convexities to and from the sun, causing thereby, a perpetual succession of day and night, summer and winter, and these migrators will be seen to follow its course, and to traverse both hemispheres from pole to pole. To those, who, contemplating this world of wonders, extend their views beyond the common gropings of mankind, it will appear, that Nature, ever provident that no part of her empire should be unoccupied, has peopled it with creatures of various kinds, and filled every corner of it with animation. To follow her into all her recesses would be an endless task ; but so far as these have been explored, every step is marked with pleasantness : and while the reflecting mind, habituated to move in its proper sphere, breaks through the trammels of pride, and removes the film of ignorance, it soars with clearer views towards perfection, and adores that Infinite Wisdom which appointed and governs the unerring course of all things.

..............................." Thus the men,
" Whom Nature's works can charm, with God himself
" Hold converse ; grow familiar day by day
" With his conceptions ; act upon his plan,
" And form to his the relish of their souls."
      Akenside's Pleasures of Imagination, Book 3, *l*. 630.

THE HERON.*

COMMON HERON, HERONSEWGH, OR HERONSHAW.

(Ardea major, Linn.—*Le Heron huppé*, Buff.)

ALTHOUGH the Heron is of a long, lank, awkward shape, yet its plumage gives it on the whole an agree-

---

* Some ornithologists have separated the Heron from the Cranes and the Storks, and from the difference observable in the conformation of their parts, consider them as a distinct genus: others, preferring the Linnæan system, class the whole together, and thus make them amount to above eighty distinct species, besides varieties, widely distributed over various parts of the globe, all differing in their size, figure, and plumage, and with talents adapted to their various places of residence, or their peculiar pursuits. But notwithstanding the difference in their bills and the colours of their plumage, the manners of all are nearly the same.

able appearance; but when stripped of its feathers, it looks as if it had been starved to death. It seldom weighs more than between three and four pounds, notwithstanding it measures about three feet in length, and in breadth, from tip to tip, above five. The bill is six inches long, straight, pointed, and strong, and its edges are thin and slightly serrated; the upper mandible is of a yellowish horn colour, darkest on the ridge; the under one yellow. A bare greenish skin is extended from the beak beyond the eyes, the irides of which are yellow, and give them a fierce and piercing aspect. The brow and crown of the head are white, bordered above the eyes by black lines which reach the nape of the neck, where they join a long flowing pendent crest of the same colour. The upper part of the neck, in some, is white, in others pale ash; the fore part, lower down, is spotted with a double row of black feathers, and those which fall over the breast are long, loose, and unwebbed; the shoulders and scapular feathers are of the same texture, of a grey colour, generally streaked with white, and spread over its down-cloathed back. The ridge of the wing is white, coverts and secondaries lead grey, bastard wings and quills bluish black, as are also the long soft feathers which take their rise on the sides under the wings, and, falling down, meet at their tips, and hide all the under parts: the latter, next the skin, are covered with a thick, matted, dirty white down, except about the belly and vent, which are almost bare. The tail is short, and consists of twelve feathers of a cinereous or brownish lead colour; the legs are dirty green, long, bare above the knees, and the middle claw is jagged on the inner edge.

The female has not the long flowing crest, or the long feathers which hang over the breast of the male, and her whole plumage is more uniformly dull and obscure. In the breeding season they congregate in large societies, and, like the Rooks, build their nests on trees, with sticks, lined with dried grass, wool, and other warm materials. The female lays from four to six eggs, of a pale greenish blue colour.*

This bird is of a melancholy deportment, a silent and patient creature; in the most severe weather it will stand

* A remarkable circumstance, with respect to these birds, occurred not long ago, at Dallam Tower, in Westmoreland, the seat of Daniel Wilson, Esq.

" There were two groves adjoining to the park : one of which, for many years, had been resorted to by a number of Herons, which there built and bred ; the other was one of the largest rookeries in the country. The two tribes lived together for a long time without any disputes. At length the trees occupied by the Herons, consisting of some very fine old oaks, were cut down in the spring of 1775, and the young brood perished by the fall of the timber. The parent birds immediately set about preparing new habitations, in order to breed again; but, as the trees in the neighbourhood of their old nests were only of a late growth, and not sufficiently high to secure them from the depredation of boys, they determined to effect a settlement in the rookery. The Rooks made an obstinate resistance ; but, after a very violent contest, in the course of which many of the Rooks, and some of their antagonists, lost their lives, the Herons at last succeeded in their attempt, built their nests, and brought out their young.

" The next season the same contests took place, which terminated like the former, by the victory of the Herons. Since that time peace seems to have been agreed upon between them : the Rooks have relinquished possession of that part of the grove which the Herons occupy ; the Herons confine themselves to those trees they first seized upon, and the two species live together in as much harmony as they did before their quarrel."—Heysham.

motionless a long time in the water, with its head laid
back between its shoulders, its bill overlapped by the
long feathers of the neck, as a defence from the cold,
and fixed to a spot, in appearance like the stump or
root of a tree, waiting for its prey, which consists of
eels and other kinds of fish, frogs, water-newts, &c.;
it is also said to devour field-mice.

The Heron traverses the country to a great distance
in quest of some convenient fishing spot, and in its aerial journies soars to a great height, to which the eye is
directed by its harsh cry, uttered from time to time
while on the wing.   In flying it draws the head between
the shoulders, and the legs stretched out, seem, like the
longer tails of some birds, to serve as a rudder.   The
motion of their wings is heavy and flagging, and yet
they get forward at a greater rate than would be imagined.

In England Herons were formerly ranked among
the royal game, and protected as such by the laws; and
whoever destroyed their eggs was liable to a penalty of
twenty shillings for each offence.   Heron hawking was
at that time a favourite diversion among the nobility and
gentry of the kingdom, at whose tables this bird was a
favourite dish, and was as much esteemed as Pheasants
and Peacocks.

THE NIGHT HERON.

LESSER ASH-COLOURED HERON, OR NIGHT RAVEN.

(Ardea Nycticorax, Linn.—*Le Bihoreau,* Buff.)

LENGTH about twenty inches. The bill is three inches and three quarters long, slightly arched, strong, and black, inclining to yellow at the base; the skin from the beak round the eyes is bare, and of a greenish colour; irides yellow. A white line is extended from the beak over each eye; a black patch, glossed with green, covers the crown of the head and nape of the neck, from which three long narrow white feathers, tipped with brown, hang loose and waving: the hinder part of the neck, coverts of the wings, the sides and tail, are ash grey; throat white; fore part of the neck, breast and belly yellowish white or buff; the back black; legs greenish yellow.

The female is nearly of the same size as the male, but she differs considerably in her plumage, which is less bright and distinct, being more blended with dirty white, brown, grey, and rusty ash, and she has not the delicate plumes which flow from the head of the male.

The Night Heron frequents the sea-shores, rivers, and inland marshes, and lives upon insects, slugs, reptiles, and fish. It remains concealed during the day, and does not roam abroad until the approach of night, when it is heard and known by its rough, harsh, and disagreeable cry, which is by some compared to the noise made by a person straining to vomit. They build on trees, and on rocky cliffs. The female lays three or four white eggs.

This species is not numerous, although widely dispersed over Europe, Asia, and America.

The above figure was taken from a stuffed specimen now in the Newcastle museum, and is the only one we have seen. The bird is indeed very uncommon in this country. Latham mentions one in the Leverian museum, which was shot not many miles from London, in May, 1782.

THE LITTLE EGRET.

(Ardea Garzetta, Linn.—*L'Aigrette,* Buff.)

THE Egret is one of the smallest, as well as the most
elegant of the Heron tribe: its shape is delicate, and
the plumage white as snow; but what constitute its
principal beauty, are the soft, silky, flowing plumes on
the head, breast, and shoulders; they consist of single
slender shafts, thinly set with pairs of fine soft threads,
which float on the slightest breath of air. Those which
arise from the shoulders are extended over the back,
and flow beyond the tail. These plumes were formerly used to decorate the helmets of warriors: they are
now applied to a gentler and better purpose, in orna-
menting the head-dresses of the European ladies, and
the turbans of the Persians and Turks.

The Egret seldom exceeds a pound and a half in weight, and rarely a foot and a half in length. A bare green skin is extended from the beak to the eyes, the irides are pale yellow: the bill and legs black. Like the common Heron they perch and build on trees, and live on the same kinds of food.

This species is found in almost every temperate and warm climate, and must formerly have been plentiful in Great Britain, if it be the same bird as that mentioned by Leland in the list or bill of fare prepared for the famous feast of Archbishop Nevil, in which one thousand of these birds were served up. No wonder the species has become nearly extinct in this country!

THE BITTERN.

BOG-BUMPER, BITTER-BUM, OR MIRE-DRUM.

(Ardea stellaris, Linn.—*Le Buior*, Buff.)

THE Bittern is nearly as large as the common Heron;
but its legs are stronger, body more plump and fleshy,
and its neck is more thickly clothed with feathers.
The beak is strong at the base, straight, sharp on the
edges, and gradually tapers to an acute point; the upper mandible is brown, the under inclining to green;
mouth wide, the gape extending beyond the eyes, with

a dusky patch at each angle: irides yellow. The crown of the head is somewhat depressed, and covered with long black feathers; throat yellowish white, sides of the neck pale rusty, variegated with black, in spotted, waved, and narrow transverse lines, and on the fore part the ground colour is whitish, and the feathers fall down in less broken and darker lengthened stripes. These neck feathers, which it can raise and depress at pleasure, are long and loose, and inclining backward, cover the neck behind; those below them on the breast, to the thighs, are streaked lengthwise with black, edged with yellowish white: the thighs, belly, and vent are dull pale yellow, clouded with dingy brown. The plumage on the back and wings is marked with black zigzag lines, bars and streaks, upon a ground shaded with rufous and yellow. The bastard wings, greater coverts, and quills are brown, barred with black. The tail, which consists of ten feathers, is very short: the legs are pale green, bare a little above the knees; the claws, particularly those on the hind toes, are long and sharp, the middle ones serrated.

The female is less than the male; her plumage is darker, and the feathers on the head, breast, and neck are shorter, and the colours not so distinctly marked. She makes an artless nest, composed chiefly of the withered stalks and leaves of the high coarse herbage, in the midst of which it is placed, and lays from four to six eggs of a greenish white.

The Bittern is a shy solitary bird; it is never seen on the wing in the day time, but sits, commonly with the head erect, hid among the reeds and rushes in the marshes, where it takes up its abode, and from whence it will not stir, unless disturbed by the sportsman. When it changes its haunts, it removes in the dusk of the evening, and then rising in a spiral direction, soars to a vast height. It flies in the same heavy manner as the Heron, and might be mistaken for that bird, were it not for the singularly resounding cry which it utters from time to time while on the wing; but this cry is feeble when compared to the hollow booming noise* which it makes during the night, in the breeding season, from its swampy retreats.

The Bittern, when attacked by the Buzzard, or other birds of prey, defends itself with great courage, and generally beats off such assailants; neither does it betray any symptoms of fear, when wounded by the sportsman, but eyes him with a keen undaunted look, and when driven to extremity, will attack him with the utmost vigour, wounding his legs, or aiming at his eyes with its sharp and piercing bill. It was formerly held in much estimation at the tables of the great.

Like the Heron, it lives upon water animals, for which it patiently watches, unmoved, for hours together.

* " The Bittern booms along the sounding marsh,
" Mixt with the cries of Heron and Mallard harsh."

THE LITTLE BITTERN.

(Ardea minuta, Linn.—*Le Blongios,* Buff.)

THE body is about the size of a Thrush. The bill
from the tip to the brow is in length one inch and se-
ven-eighths, greenish yellow, dusky at the tip of the
upper mandible, and the edges are jagged ; the feathers
on the top of the head are elongated behind; these, as
well as the back and tail are black, with greenish reflections, and the secondary and primary quills are nearly
the same; the neck is long, the hinder part of it bare
of feathers, but those from the fore part fall back and
cover it; sides of the chin dull white; the cheeks in-
cline to chesnut; the neck, lesser coverts of the wings,
lower part of the breast, and the thighs, are reddish

buff; greater coverts white; the belly and vent yellowish dirty white; the feathers on the upper part of
the breast are black, edged with pale buff, and are
spread over part of the shoulders, breast, and wings;
those below, which cover the breast to the thighs, are
long and narrowly striped down the middle with pale
brown; legs and toes dark green, and nearly of the
same length as the bill.

This species is very rarely met with in this country.
The above figure was taken from a stuffed specimen,
obligingly lent to this work by Sir M. W. Ridley, Bart.
of Blagdon, Northumberland: the bird was shot there
on the 10th of May, 1810.

THE SPOONBILL.*

WHITE SPOONBILL.

(Platalea Leucorodia, Linn.—*Le Spatule,* Buff.)

THE Spoonbill measures two feet eight inches in
length.   The whole plumage is white, though some
few have been noticed with the quills tipped with black.

* The bird we have figured would appear to have been a young
one, as the plumage of the mature male is described by Temminck to
be altogether pure white, with the exception of the breast, on which
there is a large reddish yellow patch ; the extremities of which rise in
the form of a band to the top of the back and there unite.   This patch
does not begin to appear till the second or third year.   In the female
it is very faint.

The bill, which flaps together not unlike two pieces of leather, is the most striking feature in this bird : it is six inches and a half long, broad and thick at the base, and very flat towards the extremity, where, in shape, it is widened and rounded like a spatula : it is rimmed on the edges with black, and terminated with a small downward-bent point or nib. The colour of the bill varies in different birds; in some, the little ridges which wave across the upper bill are spotted, in others striped with black or brown, and generally the ground colour of both mandibles is in different shades of deeper or lighter yellow : the insides, towards the gape of the mouth, near the edges, are studded with small hard tubercles or furrowed prominences, and are also rough near the extremities of the bill, which enables them to hold their slippery prey. A black bare skin extends from the bill round the eyes, the irides of which are grey; the skin which covers the gullet is also black and bare, and is capable of great distention. The feathers on the hinder part of the head are long and narrow, and form a sort of tuft or crest which falls behind. The toes are connected near their junction by webs, which reach the second joint of the outer toe and the first of the inner ones, and slightly border them on each side to their extremities : the feet, legs and bare part of the thighs are covered with a hard and scaly skin of a dirty black.

The White Spoonbill migrates northward in the summer, and returns south on the approach of winter, and is met with in all the intermediate low countries, between the Ferro Isles and the Cape of Good Hope. They were formerly numerous on the marshes of Sevenhuys, near Leyden, in Holland. In England they are rare visitants: Pennant mentions that a flock of them migrated into the marshes near Yarmouth in April, 1774.

Like the Rooks and the Herons, they build their nests on the tops of large trees, lay three or four eggs, the size of those of a Hen, white, sprinkled with pale red, and are very noisy during the breeding season. The intestines are described as being very long, and the *trachea arteria* like that of the Crane, and making a double inflection in the thorax.

Of the Ibis.

In this genus of birds, which is new to our work, the bill is long, thick at the base, deflected, point depressed, rounded, and obtuse; face, and sometimes the whole head naked; nostrils linear; tongue short; toes connected at the base by a membrane.

They moult once a year. The sexes do not differ except in the smaller size of the female. The plumage of the young birds is in many respects different from that of the adult.

Temminck regards as fabulous, the reputation which these birds have obtained of being great destroyers of serpents and venomous reptiles; animals which they are known never to touch.

Two species of the Ibis were held in such veneration by the ancient Egyptians, as to have been worshipped and embalmed; numerous mummies of them being found in the great sepulchres of Memphis and other cities.

THE CURLEW.

(Scolopax Arquata, Linn.—*Le Courlis,* Buff.)

THE Curlew generally measures about two feet in
length, and from tip to tip above three feet.   The bill
is about seven inches long, of a regular curve, and
tender substance at the point, which is blunt.   The
upper mandible is black, gradually softening into
brown towards the base; the under one flesh-colour-
ed.   The head and neck are streaked with darkish and
light brown; wing coverts the same; the feathers of
the back and scapulars are nearly black in the middle,
edged and deeply indented with pale rust or light grey.
The breast, belly, and lower part of the back are dull
white, the latter thinly spotted with black, the two

former with oblong strokes more thickly set, of the same colour. The quill feathers are black, the inner webs crossed or spotted with white: tail barred with black, on a white ground tinged with red : thighs bare about half way above the knees, of a bluish colour; the toes are thick, and flat on the under side, being furnished with membraneous edgings on each side to the claws.

These birds differ much in size, as well as in the different shades of their plumage, some of them weighing not more than twenty-two ounces, and others as much as thirty-seven. In the plumage of some, the white parts are, most probably from age or sex, more distinct and clear than in others, which are more uniformly grey, and tinged with pale brown.

The female is so nearly like the male, that any particular description of her is unnecessary: she makes her nest upon the ground, in a dry tuft of rushes or grass, of such withered materials as are found near, and lays four eggs of a greenish cast, spotted with brown.

The Curlew is met with in most parts of Europe, from Iceland to the Mediterranean Islands. In Britain their summer residence is upon the large, heathy, and boggy moors, where they breed. Their food consists of worms, flies, and insects, which they pick out of the soft mossy ground by the marshy pools, which are common in such places. In autumn and winter they depart to the sea-side, in great numbers, and there live upon worms, marine insects, and other fishy substances which they pick up on the beach, and among the loose rocks and pools left by the retiring tide.

THE WOODCOCK.

(Scolopax Rusticola, Linn.—*La Bécasse*, Buff.)

THE Woodcock measures fourteen inches in length,
twenty-six in breadth, and weighs about twelve ounces.
The shape of the head is remarkable, being rather ob-
tusely triangular than round, with the eyes placed near
the top, and the ears very forward, nearly on a line
with the corners of the mouth. The upper mandible,
which measures about three inches, is furrowed nearly
its whole length, and at the tip it projects beyond and
hangs over the under one, ending in a kind of knob,
which, like those of others of the same genus, is susceptible of the finest feeling, and calculated by that means,
aided, perhaps, by an acute smell, to find the small
worms in the soft moist grounds, from whence it ex-

tracts them with its sharp-pointed tongue. With the
bill it also turns over and tosses the fallen leaves in
search of insects which shelter underneath. The crown
of the head is ash colour; the nape and back part of the
neck are black, marked with three bars of rusty red: a
black line extends from the corners of the mouth to the
eyes, the orbits of which are pale buff; the whole under parts are yellowish white, numerously barred with
dark waved lines. The tail consists of twelve feathers,
which, like the quills, are black, and indented across
with reddish spots on the edges: the tip is ash above,
and glossy white below. The legs are short, feathered
to the knees, and, in some, are bluish, in others, sallow
flesh colour. The upper parts of the plumage are so
marbled, spotted, barred, streaked, and variegated, that
to describe them with accuracy would be difficult and
tedious. The colours, consisting of black, white, grey,
red, brown, rufous, and yellow, are so disposed in rows,
crossed and broken at intervals by lines and marks of
different shapes, that the whole seems to the eye, at a
little distance, blended together and confused, which
makes the bird appear exactly like the withered stalks
and leaves of ferns, sticks, moss, and grasses, which
form the back ground of the scenery by which it is sheltered in its moist and solitary retreats. The sportsman
only, by being accustomed to it, is enabled to discover
it, and his leading marks are its full dark eye, and glossy
silver-white tipped tail. The female differs very little
from the male, except in being a little larger, and less
brilliant in her colours.*

* The flesh of this bird is held in very high estimation, and hence
it is eagerly sought after by the sportsman. It is hardly necessary to

The Woodcock is migratory, and in different seasons is said to inhabit every climate: it leaves the countries bordering upon the Baltic in the autumn and setting in of winter, on its route to this country. They do not come in large flocks, but keep dropping in upon our shores singly, or sometimes in pairs, from the beginning of October till December. They must have the instinctive precaution of landing only in the night, or in dark misty weather, for they are never seen to arrive; but are frequently discovered the next morning in any ditch which affords shelter, and particularly after the extraordinary fatigue occasioned by the adverse gales which they often have to encounter in their aerial voyage. They do not remain near the shores to take their rest longer than a day, but commonly find themselves sufficiently recruited in that time to proceed inland, to the very same haunts which they left the preceding season.* In temperate weather they retire to the mossy moors, and bleak mountainous parts of the country; but as soon as the frost sets in, and the snow begins to fall, they return to lower and warmer situations, where they meet with boggy grounds and

notice, that in cooking it, the entrails are not drawn, but roasted within the bird, whence they drop out with the gravy upon slices of toasted bread, and are relished as a delicious kind of sauce.

* In the winter of 1797, the gamekeeper of E. M. Pleydell, Esq. of Whatcombe, in Dorsetshire, brought him a Woodcock, which he had caught in a net set for rabbits, alive and unhurt. Mr P. scratched the date upon a bit of thin brass, and bent it round the Woodcock's leg, and let it fly. In December the next year, Mr Pleydell shot this bird with the brass about its leg, in the very same wood where it had been first caught by the gamekeeper.

(Communicated by Sir John Trevelyan, Bart.)

springs, and little oozing mossy rills which are rarely frozen, and seek the shelter of close bushes of holly, furze, and brakes in the woody glens, or hollow dells which are covered with underwood : there they remain concealed during the day, and remove to different haunts, and feed only in the night. From the beginning of March to the end, or sometimes to the middle of April, they draw towards the coasts, and avail themselves of the first fair wind to return to their native woods : should it happen to continue long to blow adversely, they are thereby detained; and as their numbers increase, they are more easily found and destroyed by the merciless sportsman.

The female makes her nest on the ground, generally at the root or stump of a decayed tree; it is carelessly formed of dried fibres and leaves, upon which she lays four or five eggs, larger than those of a Pigeon, of a rusty grey, blotched and marked with dusky spots. The young leave the nest as soon as they are freed from the shell, but the parents continue to attend and assist them until they can provide for themselves. Buffon says they sometimes take a weak one under their throat, and convey it more than a thousand paces.*

* Latham mentions three varieties of British Woodcocks: in the first, the head is of a pale red, body white, and the wings brown ; the second is of a dun, or rather cream colour; and the third of a pure white. Dr Heysham, in his Catalogue of Cumberland Animals, mentions his having met with one, the general colour of which was a fine pale ash, with frequent bars of a very delicate rufous : tail brown, tipped with white ; and the bill and legs flesh colour. In addition to these, some other varieties are taken notice of by the late Marmaduke Tunstall, Esq. of Wycliffe, in his interleaved books of ornithology.

Latham and Pennant assert, that some Woodcocks deviate from the course which nature seems to have taught their species, by remaining throughout the year, and breeding in this country; and this assertion Mr Tunstall corroborates by such a number of well-authenticated instances, that the fact is unquestionable.*

When the Woodcock is pursued by the sportsman, its flight is very rapid, but short, as it drops behind the

A white Woodcock was seen three successive winters in Penrice wood, near Penrice Castle, in Glamorganshire: it was repeatedly flushed and shot at during that time, in the very same place where it was first discovered: at last it was found dead, with several others which had perished by the severity of the weather, in the winter of 1793. This account, which was communicated to the author by Sir John Trevelyan, Bart. on the authority of the Rev. Dr Hunt, proves not only the existence of white Woodcocks, but also the truth of the assertion, that the haunts of this bird are the same year after year.

* To describe the various methods which are practised by fowlers to catch this bird, would be tedious; but it may not be improper to notice those most commonly in use, and against which it does not seem to be equally on its guard as against the gun. It is easily caught in nets, traps, and springes which are placed in its accustomed runs or paths, as its suspicions are all lulled into security by the silence of the night; and it will not fly or leap over any obstacles which are placed in its way, while in quest of its food; therefore, in those places, barriers and avenues formed of sticks, stones, &c. are constructed so as to *weir* it into the fatal openings, where it is entrapped: in like manner, a low fence made of the tops of broom stuck into the ground, across the wet furrow of a field, or a runner from a spring which is not frozen, is sufficient to stay its progress, and to make it seek from side to side for an opening through which it might pass; and there it seldom escapes the noose that is set to secure it.

At the root of the first quill in each wing is a small pointed narrow feather, very elastic, and much sought after by painters, by whom it is used as a pencil. A feather of a similar kind is found in the whole

first suitable sheltering coppice, with great suddenness, and in order to elude discovery, runs swiftly off, in quest of some place where it may hide itself in greater security.

of this tribe, and also in every one of the Tringas and Plovers which the author has examined.

THE SNIPE.

SNITE, OR HEATHER-BLEATER.

(Scolopax Gallinago, Linn.—*La Bécassine,* Buff.)

THE Snipe is generally about four ounces in weight, twelve inches in length, and fourteen in breadth. The bill is nearly three inches long; in some pale brown, in others greenish yellow, rather flat and dark at the tip, and very smooth in the living bird; but it soon becomes dimpled like the end of a thimble, after the bird is dead: the head is divided lengthwise by three reddish or rusty white lines, and two of black; one of the former passes along the middle of the crown, and one above each eye: a darkish mark is extended from the corners of the mouth nearly to each eye, and the auriculars form spots of the same colour: the chin and fore part of the neck are yellowish white, the former plain, the latter spotted with brown. The scapulars are elegantly striped lengthwise on one web, and barred on the other, with black and yellow: quills dusky, the edge of the primaries, and tips of the secondaries, white; those next to the back barred with black, and pale rufous: the breast and belly are white: the tail coverts are reddish brown, and so long as to cover the greater part of it; the tail consists of fourteen feathers, the webs of which, as far as they are concealed by the coverts, are dusky, thence downward, tawny or rusty orange, and irregularly marked or crossed with black. The tip is commonly of a pale reddish yellow, but in some specimens nearly white: the legs are pale green.*

The common residence of the Snipe is in small bogs or wet grounds, where it is almost constantly digging and nibbling in the soft mud, in search of its food, which consists chiefly of a very small red transparent worm, about half an inch long; it is said also to eat slugs, insects, and grubs, which breed in great abundance in those slimy stagnant places. In these retreats, when undisturbed, the Snipe walks leisurely, with its head erect, and at short intervals keeps moving the tail. But in this state of tranquillity it is very rarely to be seen, as it is extremely watchful, and perceives the sportsman or his dog at a great distance, and instantly conceals itself among the variegated withered herbage,

* Mr Tunstall mentions a " very curious pied Snipe which was shot in Bottley meadow, near Oxford, September 8, 1789, by a Mr Court: its throat, breast, back, and wings, were beautifully covered or streaked with white, and on its forehead was a star of the natural colour; it had also a ring round the neck and the tail, with the tips of the wings of the same colour."

so similar in appearance to its own plumage, that it is almost impossible to discover it while squatted motionless in its seat : it seldom, however, waits the near approach of any person, particularly in open weather, but commonly springs, and takes flight at a distance beyond the reach of the gun.   When first disturbed, it utters a kind of feeble whistle, and generally flies against the wind, turning nimbly in a zigzag direction for two or three hundred paces, and sometimes soaring almost out of sight; its note is then something like the bleating of a goat, but this is changed to a singular humming or drumming noise, uttered in its descent.

From its vigilance and manner of flying, it is one of the most difficult birds to shoot.   Some sportsmen can imitate their cries, and by that means draw them within reach of their shot; others, of a less honourable description, prefer the more certain method of catching them in the night by a springe like that which is used for the Woodcock.

The Snipe is migratory, and is met with in all countries : like the Woodcock, it shuns the extremes of heat and cold, by keeping upon the bleak moors in summer, and seeking the shelter of the vallies in winter.   In severe frosts and storms of snow, driven by the extremity of the weather, they seek the unfrozen boggy places, runners from springs, or any open streamlet of water, and they are sure to be found, often in considerable numbers, in these places, where they sometimes sit till nearly trodden upon before they will take flight.

Although it is well known that numbers of Snipes leave Great Britain in the spring, and return in the autumn, yet it is equally well ascertained, that many

constantly remain and breed in various parts of the
country, for their nests and young ones have been so
often found as to leave no doubt of this fact. The female makes her nest in the most retired and inaccessible part of the morass, generally under the stump of an
alder or willow : it is composed of withered grasses and
a few feathers : her eggs, four or five in number, are of
an oblong shape, and greenish, with rusty spots. The
young ones run off soon after they are freed from the
shell, but they are attended by the parents until their
bills have acquired a sufficient firmness to enable them
to provide for themselves.*

* The Snipe is a very fat bird, but its fat does not cloy, and very
rarely disagrees even with the weakest stomach. It is much esteemed as a delicious and well-flavoured dish, and is cooked in the same
manner as the Woodcock.

THE JUDCOCK.

JACK SNIPE, GID, OR JETCOCK.

(Scolopax Gallinula, Linn.—*La petite Bécassine,* Buff.)

THE Judcock, in its figure and plumage, nearly resembles the Snipe; but it is only about half its weight,
seldom exceeding two ounces, or measuring more in
length than eight inches and a half.   The bill is black
at the tip, and light towards the base, and rather more
than an inch and a half in length.   A black streak divides the head lengthwise from the base of the bill to
the nape of the neck; and another, of a yellowish colour, passes over each eye to the hinder part of the
head: in the midst of this, above the eye, is a narrow
black stripe running parallel with the top of the head
from the crown to the nape.   The neck is white, spotted
with brown and pale red.   The scapulars and tertials
are very long and beautiful; on their exterior edges

they are bordered with a stripe of yellow, and the inner webs are streaked and marked with bright rust on a deep brown, or rather bronze, ground, reflecting in different lights a shining purple or green. The quills are dusky. The rump is glossy violet or bluish purple; the belly and vent white. The tail consists of twelve pointed feathers of a dark brown, edged with rust colour: the legs are of a dirty or dull green.

The Judcock is of nearly the same character as the Snipe; it feeds upon the same kinds of food, lives and breeds in the same swamps and marshes, and conceals itself from the sportsman with as great circumspection, among the rushes or tufts of coarse grass. It, however, differs in this particular, that it seldom rises from its lurking place until it is almost trampled upon, and, when flushed, does not fly to so great a distance. It is as much esteemed as the Snipe, and is cooked in the same manner.

The eggs are not larger than those of a Lark; in other respects they are very like those of the Snipe.

THE GODWIT.

COMMON GODWIT, GODWYN, YARWHELP, OR YARWIP.

(Scolopax Ægocephala, Linn.—*La grande Barge grise*, Buff.)

THE weight of this bird is about twelve ounces ; length about sixteen inches. Bill four inches long, and bent a little upwards, black at the point, gradually softening into a pale purple towards the base ; a whitish streak passes from the bill over each eye : the head, neck, back, scapulars, and coverts, are dingy reddish pale brown, each feather marked down the middle with a dark spot. The fore part of the breast is streaked with black ; belly, vent, and tail white, the latter regularly barred with black : the webs of the first six quill feathers black, edged on the interior sides with reddish brown: legs in general dark coloured, inclining to greenish blue.

The Godwit is met with in various parts of Europe, Asia, and America: in Great Britain, in the spring and summer, it resides in the fens and marshes, where it rears its young, and feeds upon small worms and insects. During these seasons it removes only from one marsh to another; but when the winter sets in with severity, it seeks the salt marshes and sea-shores.*

* The Godwit is much esteemed, by epicures, as a great delicacy, and sells very high. It is caught in nets, to which it is allured by a *stale*, or stuffed bird, in the same manner, and in the same season, as the Ruffs and Reeves.

Of the Sandpiper.

THE tongue is slender; in some the toes divided, in others the outer and middle toe connected as far as the first joint by a membrane; hinder toe weak : their bills are nearly of the same form as those of the preceding genus, but shorter, and slightly inclined downwards : their haunts and manner of life are also very similar. Latham has enumerated thirty-seven species and nine varieties of this genus, seventeen of which are British, exclusive of those which in this work are placed among the Plovers; but the history and classification of this genus are involved in much uncertainty.

They moult twice a year, at stated periods; the winter and summer plumage varying very much; the principal colours commonly changing from white to red, and from ash to black. The young, previous to the first moult, differ greatly from the old birds. The sexes are distinguished by their size only, the female being generally the largest.

Scapular feather of the Woodcock.

THE LAPWING,

PEE-WIT, BASTARD PLOVER, OR TE-WIT.

(Tringa vanellus, Linn.—*Le Vanneau,* Buff.)

Is about the size of a Pigeon. Bill black; eyes
large and hazel; top of the head black, glossed with
green; a tuft of long narrow feathers issues from the
back part of the head, and turns upwards at the end;
some of them four inches in length: sides of the head
and neck white; which is interrupted by a blackish
streak above and below the eye; back part of the neck
very pale brown; fore part, and the breast, black;
back and the wing coverts dark green, glossed with
purple and blue reflections; quills black, the first four
tipped with white; breast and belly pure white; upper
tail coverts and vent pale chesnut; tail white at the

base, the rest of it black, with pale tips, outer feathers almost wholly white: legs red; claws black; hind claw very short.

This bird is a constant inhabitant of this country; but as it subsists chiefly on worms, it is forced to change its place in quest of food, and is frequently seen in great numbers by the sea-shores, where it finds an abundant supply. It is every where well known by its loud and incessant cries, which it repeats without intermission whilst on the wing, and from which in most languages a name has been given to it, imitative of the sound. The Pee-wit is a lively, active bird, almost continually in motion; it sports and frolics in the air in all directions, and assumes a variety of attitudes; it remains long upon the wing, and sometimes rises to a considerable height; it runs along the ground very nimbly, and springs and bounds from spot to spot with great agility. The female lays four eggs, of a dirty olive, spotted with black: she makes no nest, but deposits them upon a little dry grass hastily scraped together: the young birds run very soon after they are hatched: during this period the old ones are very assiduous in their attention to their charge; on the approach of any person to the place of their deposit, they flutter round his head with cries of the greatest inquietude, which increase as he draws nearer the spot where the brood are squatted; in case of extremity, and as a last resource, they run along the ground as if lame, in order to draw off the attention of the fowler from any further pursuit. The young Lapwings are first covered with a blackish down interspersed with long white hairs, which they gradually lose, and about the latter end of July they acquire their beautiful plumage. At this time they assemble in flocks, which hover in the air, saunter in the meadows, and after rain, disperse among the ploughed fields. In October the Lapwings are very fat, and are then said to be excellent eating. Their eggs are considered as a great delicacy, and are sold in London at three shillings a dozen.

The following anecdote communicated by the late Rev. J. Carlyle, vicar of Newcastle, is worthy of notice, as it shews the domestic nature of this bird, as well as the art with which it conciliates the regard of animals differing from itself in nature, and generally considered as hostile to every species of the feathered tribe. Two of these birds, given to Mr Carlyle, were put into a garden, where one of them soon died; the other continued to pick up such food as the place afforded, till winter deprived it of its usual supply: necessity soon compelled it to draw nearer the house, by which it gradually became familiarised to occasional interruptions from the family. At length a servant, when she had occasion to go into the back-kitchen with a light, observed that the Lapwing always uttered his cry ' *pee-wit*' to obtain admittance. He soon grew more familiar; as the winter advanced, he approached as far as the kitchen, but with much caution, as that part of the house was generally inhabited by a dog and a cat, whose friendship the Lapwing at length conciliated so entirely, that it was his regular custom to resort to the fire-side as soon as it grew dark, and spend the evening and night with his two associates, sitting close by them, and partaking of the comforts of a warm fire-side. As soon as spring appeared, he left off coming to the house,

and betook himself to the garden; but on the approach
of winter, he had recourse to his old shelter and his old
friends, who received him very cordially.   Security
was productive of insolence; what was at first obtained
with caution, was afterwards taken without reserve: he
frequently amused himself with washing in the bowl
which was set for the dog to drink out of, and while
he was thus employed, he shewed marks of the greatest
indignation if either of his companions presumed to in-
terrupt him.   He died in the asylum he had chosen,
being choaked with something he had picked up from
the floor.   During his confinement, crumbs of wheaten
bread were his principal food, which he preferred to
any thing else.

THE GREEN SANDPIPER.

(Tringa Ochropus, Linn.—*Le Becasseau, ou Cul-blanc,*
Buff.)

THIS bird measures about ten inches in length, to
the end of the toes nearly twelve, and weighs about
three ounces and a half. The bill is black, and an
inch and a half long: a pale streak extends from it
over each eye; between which and the corners of the
mouth, there is a dusky patch. The crown of the
head and hinder part of the neck are dingy brownish
ash, in some narrowly streaked with white: throat
white: fore part of the neck mottled or streaked with
brown spots, on a white or pale ash ground. The
whole upper parts of the plumage glossy bronze, or
olive brown, elegantly marked on the edge of each
feather with small roundish white spots: the quills are
without spots, and of a darker brown: the secondaries
and tertials very long: insides of the wings dusky,

edged with white grey; inside coverts next the body curiously barred, from the shaft of each feather to the edge, with narrow white lines, formed nearly of the shape of two sides of a triangle.   Belly, vent, tail coverts, and tail, white; the last broadly barred with black, the middle feathers having four bars, and those next to them decreasing in the number of bars towards the outside feathers, which are quite plain : legs green.

This bird is not any where numerous, and is of a solitary disposition, seldom more than a pair being seen together, and that chiefly in the breeding season.   It is scarce in England, but is said to be more common in the northern parts of the globe, even as far as Iceland.   It is reported that they never frequent the sea-shores, but their places of abode are commonly on the margins of the lakes in the interior and mountainous parts of the country.

THE KNOT.

KNUTE, OR KNOUT.

(Tringa Canatus, Linn.—*Le Canut,* Buff.)

THESE birds, which seem to be a connecting link between the Scolopax and Tringa genera, differ considerably from each other in their appearance, in different
seasons of the year, as well as from age and sex. The
specimen from which the above drawing was taken,
measured from the point of the bill to the tip of the
tail, eight inches and a half, the extended wings about
fifteen, and it weighed two ounces eight drachms : bill
one inch and three-eighths long, black at the tip, and
dusky, fading into orange towards the base; tongue
of nearly the same length, sharp and horny at the
point; sides of the head, neck, and breast, cinereous,
edged with ash grey; chin white, and a stroke of the
same passed over each eye. All the upper parts of the

plumage darkish brown, but more deep and glossy on
the crown of the head, back and scapulars, and each
feather edged with ash or grey; under parts cream coloured white, streaked or spotted with brown on the
sides and vent; greater coverts of the wings tipped with
white, forming a bar across them when extended: legs
reddish yellow, and short, not measuring more than
two inches and one-eighth from the middle toe nail to
the knee: thighs feathered very nearly to the knees;
toes divided without any connecting membrane.

These birds are caught in Lincolnshire and the other
fenny counties, in great numbers,* by nets, into which
it is decoyed by carved wooden figures, painted to represent itself, and placed within them, much in the same
way as the Ruff. It is also fattened for sale, and esteemed by many equal to the Ruff in the delicacy of its flavour. The season for taking it is from August to November, after which the frost compels it to disappear.

This bird is said to have been a favourite dish with
Canute, king of England; and Camden observes, that
its name is derived from his—Knute, or Knout, as he
was called, which, in process of time, has been changed
to Knot.

* Pennant says fourteen dozen have been taken at once.

THE RED-LEGGED SANDPIPER.

(Tringa Bewickii,* Montagu.)

THIS bird measures from the tip of the beak to the
end of the tail, ten inches. The bill is an inch and
three-eighths long, black at the tip, and reddish towards the base: crown of the head spotted with dark
brown, disposed in streaks, and edged with pale brown
and grey: a darkish patch covers the space between
the corners of the mouth and the eyes: chin white:
brow and cheeks pale brown, prettily freckled with
small dark spots: hinder part of the neck composed of
a mixture of pale brown, grey and ash, with a few indistinct dusky spots; fore part, and breast white, clouded with a dull cinnamon colour, and sparingly and ir-

---

* Although Montagu has done us the honor to name this bird
Tringa Bewickii, we have some reason to suspect that it may prove
to be the Ruff in one of its many diversified states of plumage.

regularly marked with black spots, reflecting a purple gloss: shoulder and scapular feathers black, edged with pale rust, and having the same glossy reflections as those on the breast: tertials nearly of the same length as the quills, and marked like the first annexed figure: ridges of the wings brownish ash; coverts, back, and rump nearly the same, but inclining to olive, and the middle of each feather of a deeper dusky brown: primary quills deep olive brown: exterior webs of the secondaries also of that colour, but lighter, edged and tipped with white, and the inner webs are mostly white towards the base: tail coverts glossy black, edged with pale rust, and tipped with white; but in some of them a streak of white passes from the middle upwards, nearly the whole length, as in the second figure. The tail feathers are lightish brown, except the two middle ones, which are barred with large spots of a darker hue: the belly and vent white: legs bare above the knees, and red as sealing wax; claws black. The female is less than the male, and her plumage more dingy and indistinct: an egg taken out of her previous to stuffing, was surprisingly large, considering her bulk, being about the size of that of a Magpie, of a greenish white colour, spotted and blotched with brown, of a long shape, and pointed at the smaller end.

The foregoing figure and description were taken from a pair, male and female, which were shot on Rippengale fen, in Lincolnshire, on the 14th of May, 1799, by Major Charles Dilke, of the Warwickshire cavalry, who also obligingly pointed out several leading features of these birds, in which they differ materially from the *Scolopax Calidris* of Linnæus, called here the Redshank or Poolsnipe. He says, " this bird is a constant inhabitant of the fens, and is known to sportsmen by its singular notes, which are very loud and melodious, and are heard even when the bird is beyond the reach of sight."

The description of this bird (which, it seems, is common in the fen countries) has been more particularly attended to, because it has not been noticed in any of the popular works on ornithology; at least, not so accurately as to enable a naturalist to distinguish it by the proper name. Annexed are the scapular and tail feathers of this bird.

THE PURRE,*

(Tringa Cinclus, Linn.—*L'Alouette de Mer,* Buff.)

MEASURES about seven inches and a half in length,
and in breadth about fourteen; but sometimes rather
more. The bill is black, grooved on the sides of the
upper mandible, and about an inch and a quarter in
length: tongue nearly the same length, sharp and hard
at the point: a whitish line runs from the brow over
each eye, and a brownish one from the sides of the
mouth to the eyes, and over the cheeks: the fore part
of the neck is pale ash, mottled with brown: the head,
hinder part of the neck, upper part of the back, and
the scapulars, are brownish ash, but the middle of the
feathers on these parts is dark brown; hence there is
a more or less mottled and streaked appearance in different birds. The scapular feathers, next the back, are

* In the north of England these birds are called Stints, in other
parts, the Least Snipe, Ox-Bird, Ox-Eye, Bull's-Eye, Sea-Lark, and
Wagtail.

deep brown, edged with bright ferruginous; tertials, rump, and tail coverts nearly the same: bastard wing, primary and secondary quills, deep brown: lesser coverts brown, edged with yellowish white: greater coverts of nearly the same colour, but tipped with white: throat, breast, belly, and vent, white: the two middle feathers of the tail dusky: the rest ash: legs, thighs, and toes black, inclining to green. The female has not the bright ferruginous-edged feathers on the upper scapulars, and her whole plumage is more uniformly of a brownish ash, mixed with grey.

The Purre, with others of the same genus, appears in great numbers on the sea-shores, in various parts of Great Britain, during the winter season: they run nimbly near the edges of the flowing and retiring waves, and are almost perpetually wagging their tails, whilst they are at the same time busily employed in picking up their food, which consists chiefly of small worms and insects. On taking flight, they give a kind of scream, and skim along near the surface of the water with great rapidity, as well as with great regularity: they do not fly directly forward, but perform their evolutions in large semi-circles, alternately in their sweep approaching the shore and the sea, and the curvature of their course is pointed out by the flocks appearing suddenly and alternately in a dark or in a snowy white colour, as their backs or their bellies are turned to or from the spectator.*

* It is somewhat remarkable that birds of different species, such as the Ring-Dotterel, Sanderling, &c. which associate with the Purre, Dunlin, &c. should understand the signal, which, from their wheel-

The Purre leaves this country in the spring, but whither it retires to breed is not yet known. It is said to be widely dispersed over both Europe and America.

By the kindness of his friends the author has been furnished with many of these birds; and on the most minute inspection, as has before been noticed in respect of others of this genus, they all differed in a greater or less degree from each other.*

ing about altogether, with such promptitude and good order, it would appear is given to the whole flock.

* In a variety of this species, obligingly presented by George Strickland, Esq. of Ripon, the bill was bent a little downward; and the fore part of the neck and the breast were of a pale reddish buff colour: in other respects it did not differ materially.

THE LITTLE STINT.

LITTLE SANDPIPER, OR LEAST SNIPE.

(Tringa pusilla, Linn.—*La petite Alouette de Mer,*
Brisson.)

THIS bird, the least of the Sandpiper tribe, nearly
resembles the last species.　It weighs twelve penny-
weights troy ; length nearly six inches; breadth rather
more than eleven; the bill, to the corners of the mouth,
is five-eighths of an inch.　The feathers on the crown of
the head are black, edged with rusty : it is marked, like
most of the genus, by a light streak over each eye, and
a dark spot below and before them : the throat, fore
part of the neck, and belly are white ; and the breast
is tinged with pale reddish yellow : the shoulders and
scapulars black, edged with white on the exterior webs
of each feather, and on the interior with rust : back and
tail dusky : legs slender, and nearly black.*

* Our bird was shot by Robert Pearson, Esq. of Newcastle, on the
10th of September, 1801.

THE TURNSTONE.

SEA DOTTEREL, OR HEBRIDAL SANDPIPER.

(Tringa Interpres, Linn.—*Le Coulon-chaud,* Buff.)

THIS is a plump-made, and prettily variegated bird, and measures about eight inches and a quarter in length. The bill is black, straight, strong, and not more than an inch in length: the ground colour of the head and neck white, with small spots on the crown and hinder parts; a black stroke crosses the forehead to the eyes: the auriculars are formed by a patch of the same colour, which, pointing forward to the corners of the mouth, and falling down, is spread over the sides of the breast, whence ascends another branch, which, like a band, goes about the lower part of the neck behind.* The back, scapulars, and tertials are

---

* In some specimens the lower part of the neck is white.

black, edged with rusty red: lesser coverts of the wings cinereous brown; greater coverts black, edged with ferruginous, and tipped with white: primary and secondary quills black, the latter white at the ends: rump and tail coverts white, crossed with a black bar: tail black, tipped with white: fore part of the breast, belly, and vent white: thighs feathered nearly to the knees: legs and feet red. This and the succeeding bird are now said to be the same species, and differing only from age or sex. It is quite obvious that it ought to be separated from the genus Tringa, to which it bears little affinity. Temminck has done so, and formed it into a new genus (Strepsilas).

THE TURNSTONE.

(Tringa Morinella, Linn.—*Le Coulon-chaud cendré,*
Buff.)

This is like the preceding in size and shape. The
bill is short, strong, thick at the base, and of a dark
horn-colour, tinged with red: the crown and hinder
part of the head are dusky, edged with greyish brown;
the fore part, from the eyes to the bill, pale brown; a
curved patch or band of the latter colour bounds the
lower part of the neck, points forward, and falls down
towards the points of the wings; between this band and
the head, is a demi-ring of brownish black, which nearly surrounds the neck, a branch from which strikes upwards to the corners of the mouth, and another falls
down, forming a kind of inverted gorget on the fore
part of the neck, and sides of the breast: the colour of
the throat is white, which tapers to a point on the fore
part of the neck: upper parts of the plumage dusky,

edged with rusty or brownish red; but some of the scapulars next to the wings are partly edged with white: tertials long, and deeply edged and tipped with a fine pale rufous brown: ridge of the wings and bastard quills brownish black: lesser coverts adjoining the ridge, white: primaries and secondaries, black,—the bases of the former, and tips of the latter, white; the greater coverts are also deeply tipped with white, which, when the wing is extended, forms a bar quite across it: the under parts of the plumage, the back, and tail coverts are white, excepting a black patch which crosses the rump. The tail consists of twelve black feathers, tipped with white, except the two middle ones, which are entirely black: legs and toes short, and orange red. The male excels the female in the beauty of his plumage; her pyebald marks are not so distinct, and her colours are uniformly more dull and confused.

Turnstones frequent the sea-shores in various parts of Great Britain, and have obtained their name from their manner of turning over small stones in quest of their prey, which consists of small marine insects, worms, and bivalve shell-fish.

This bird is chiefly confined to the northern, as is the former to the southern parts of Great Britain.

Of the Avoset.

BILL very long, slender, weak, depressed throughout; the point flexible, and bending considerably upwards; nostrils narrow pervious, and linear; tongue
short: legs very long; feet much palmated, the webs
deeply indented from the nails towards their middle;
back toe placed high, and very small.

The Avoset is migratory, and is met with in temperate climates, on the shores in various parts of Europe.

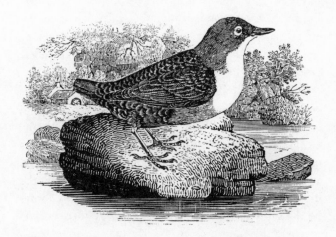

THE WATER OUZEL.

WATER CROW, DIPPER, OR WATER PIOT.

(Sturnus Cinclus, Linn.—*Le Merle d'Eau,* Buff.)

THE length of the Water Ouzel is about seven inches
and a half from the point of the beak to the end of its
tail, which is very short, and gives the bird a thick and
stumpy appearance. The mouth is wide; the bill black,
about three quarters of an inch long; the upper mandible rather hollow in the middle, and bent a little
downwards at the point; orbits white, irides hazel.
The upper parts of the head and of the neck are deepish rusty brown; the back, rump, scapulars, wing coverts, belly, vent, and tail are black; but each feather
on these parts is distinctly edged with hoary grey.
The breast, fore part of the neck and throat are of a
snowy white; and the black and white on the belly

and breast are separated by a rusty brown. The legs and toes are short and strong, the scales pale blue, the hinder part and joints brown; the claws are curved, and the toes are distinctly parted, without any membrane between to join them.

This solitary species is removed from the place it has hitherto holden, in all systems among the land birds: it ought not to be classed any longer with the Ouzels and Thrushes, to which it bears no affinity. Its manners and habits are also different from those birds, and are peculiar to itself. It is chiefly found in the high and mountainous parts of the country, and always by the sides of brooks and rocky rivers, but particularly where they fall in cascades, or run with great rapidity among stones and fragments of broken rocks; there it may be seen perched on the top of a stone in the midst of a torrent, in a continual dipping motion, or short courtesy often repeated, whilst watching for its food, which consists of small fishes and insects. The feathers, like those of the Duck tribe, are impervious to water, whereby it is enabled to continue a long time in that fluid without sustaining injury. But the most singular trait in its character, is that of its possessing the power of walking, in quest of its prey, on the pebbly bottom of a river, and with the same ease, as on dry land.*

* Being from its specific gravity much lighter than water, the circumstance of its walking so easily at the bottom of the water is doubted. Montagu admits his having seen it, but says it appeared to tumble about in a very extraordinary manner, with its head downwards, as if pecking something; and at the same time using great exertion with both its wings and legs.

The female makes her nest in the banks of a rivulet, sometimes behind a water fall when it overshoots a steep rock, and thus leaves a vacuum: it is nearly of the same form as that of a common Wren; she lays four or five eggs, which are white, lightly blushed with red.

THE KINGFISHER.

(Alcedo ispida, Linn.—*Le Martin-pêcheur,* Buff.)

This splendid little bird is of rather a clumsy shape,
the head being large in proportion to the size of the
body, and the legs and feet very small. The length is
only seven inches, breadth eleven; weight about two
ounces and a quarter. The bill, measured from the
corners of the mouth, is two inches long, vertically
compressed on the sides, strong, straight, and tapering
to a sharp point : the upper mandible is black, fading
into red towards the base; the under one, as well as
the inside of the mouth, reddish orange : irides hazel,
inclining to red. A broad stripe passes from the bill
over the eye to the hinder part of the neck, of a bright
orange, but margined on the side of the mouth, and
crossed below the eye, by a narrow black stroke, and
terminated behind the auriculars with a slanting wedge-

shaped white spot. The throat is white; the head, and the wing coverts are a deep shining green, spotted with bright light blue: the scapulars and exterior webs of the quills are of the same colour, but without spots. The middle of the back, the rump, and coverts of the tail are of a most resplendent azure: the tail, which consists of twelve short feathers, is deep rich blue, and the whole under part of the body, bright orange. The legs and toes are red, and are peculiar in their shape and conformation, the three forward toes being unconnected from the claws to the first joints, from whence they appear as if grown into each other; and the inner and hinder ones are placed in a line on the inside of the foot, whereby the heel is widened, and seems pressed out.

It is difficult to conceive why ornithologists have classed the Kingfisher with land birds, as its habits and manner of living are wholly confined to the fresh waters, on the margins of which it will sit for hours together on a projecting twig, or stone; at one while fluttering its wings, and exposing its brilliant plumage to the sun; at another, hovering in the air like the Kestril, it waits the moment when it may seize its prey, on which it darts almost unerringly: often it remains for several seconds under water, before it has gained the object of its pursuit, then brings up the little fish, which it carries to the land, beats to death, and swallows.

The female commonly makes her nest by the sides of rivers or brooks, in a hole made by the mole, or the water-rat: this she enlarges or contracts to suit her purpose; and it is conjectured, from the difficulty of finding the nest, that frequently the hole which leads to it is under water. The eggs are clear white.

To notice the many strange and contradictory accounts of this bird, as well as of its nest, transmitted to us by the ancients,* and to enumerate the properties ascribed to it by the superstitious in all ages, would occupy too large a portion of this work : but the following modern instance seems worthy of notice:—

Dr Heysham, of Carlisle, in his Catalogue of Cumberland Animals, says, " On the 7th of May a boy from Upperby brought me a Kingfisher alive, which he had taken when sitting on her eggs the night before: from him I received the following information :— Having often this spring observed these birds frequent a bank upon the river Peteril, he watched them carefully, and saw them go into a small hole in the bank. The hole was too small to admit his hand, but as it was made in the soft mould, he easily enlarged it. It was upwards of half a yard long; at the end of it the eggs, which were six in number, were placed upon the bare mould, there being not the smallest appearance of a nest."

---

* Their nests are wonderful—of the figure of a ball rather elevated, with a very narrow mouth; they look like a large sponge : they cannot be cut with a knife, but may be broken with a smart stroke : they have the appearance of petrified sea-froth. It is not discovered of what they are formed; some think of Prickly-back bones, since they live upon fish.—*Pliny.*

Aristotle compares the nest to a gourd, and its substance and texture to those sea-balls or lumps of interwoven filaments which are cut with difficulty; but, when dried, become friable.

Ælian and *Plutarch* describe it as being made to float on the placid face of the ocean.

Kingfishers are not so numerous as might be expected from the number of eggs found in their nests, owing probably to the young being destroyed by the floods, which must often rise above the level of the holes where they are bred.

Except in the breeding season, this bird is usually seen alone, flying near the surface of the water with the rapidity of an arrow, like a little brilliant meteor, by which appearance the eye is enabled to follow its long-continued course. Considering the shortness of its wings, the velocity with which it flies is surprising.

Ornithologists inform us that Kingfishers are found in almost every part of the globe; but it does not appear that more than this one species has ever been seen in Europe.

THE WATER RAIL.

BILCOCK, VELVET RUNNER, OR BROOK OUZEL.

(Rallus aquaticus, Linn.—*Le Rale d'Eau,* Buff.)

THIS bird, though a distinct genus of itself, has many traits in its character very similar to both the Land Rail and the Spotted Rail: it is migratory, like the former, to which it also bears some resemblance in size, lengthened shape, and compressed body; its haunts and manner of living are nearly the same as those of the latter; but it differs from both in the length of its bill, and in its plumage. It weighs about four ounces and a half, and measures twelve inches in length and sixteen in breadth. The bill is slightly curved, and one inch and three quarters long; the upper mandible dusky, edged with red; the under reddish orange; irides red. The top of the head, hinder part of the neck, the back, scapulars, coverts of the wings, and tail, are black, edged with dingy brown; the ridge of the wings is white, the bastard wing barred with white, the inside barred with brown and white, and the quills and secondaries dusky; the side feathers are beautifully crossed with black and white, and slightly tipped with pale reddish brown. The inner side of the thighs, the belly, and the vent are pale brown, and in some specimens, speckled with bluish ash. The sides of the head, the chin,* fore part of the neck, and the breast, are dark hoary lead colour, slightly tinged with pale rufous. The tail consists of twelve short black feathers, edged and tipped with dirty red; some of those on the under side barred with black and white. The legs, which are placed far behind, are a dull dingy red; toes long, and without any connecting membrane. Latham says, " the eggs are more than an inch and a half long, of a pale yellowish colour, marked all over with dusky brown spots, nearly equal in size, but irregular."

The Water Rail is a shy and solitary bird. Its constant abode is in low wet places, much overgrown with sedges, reeds, and other coarse herbage, among which it shelters and feeds in hidden security. It runs, occasionally flirting up its tail, through its tracts, with the same swiftness as the Land Rail runs through the meadows and corn fields, shews as great an aversion to taking flight as that bird, and has more of the means in its power of disappointing the sportsman. It generally exhausts his patience, and distracts and misleads his dog, by the length of time to which it can protract

* The chin in some specimens is cream coloured.

its taking wing; and it seldom rises until it has crossed
every pool, and run through every avenue within the
circuit of its retreats.   It is, however, easily shot when
flushed, for it flies but indifferently, with its legs dang-
ling down.   It is not very common in Great Britain,
but is numerous in the marshes of the northern countries of Europe, whence, partially and irregularly, it
migrates southward, even into Africa, during the severity of the winter season.   Buffon says, " they pass
Malta in the spring and autumn," and to confirm this,
adds, " that the Viscount de Querhoënt saw a flight of
them at the distance of fifty leagues from the coasts of
Portugal on the 17th of April, some of which were so
fatigued that they suffered themselves to be caught by
the hand."   The flesh of the Water Rail is not so generally esteemed as that of the Land Rail, and yet by
many it is thought rich and delicious eating.

THE COMMON GALLINULE.

WATER HEN, OR MOOR HEN.

(Gallinula chloropus, Lath.—*La Poule d'Eau,* Buff.)

THE weight of this bird varies from ten and a half
to fifteen ounces: the length from the tip of the beak
to the end of the tail is about fourteen inches, the
breadth twenty-two. The bill is rather more than an
inch long, of a greenish yellow at the tip, and reddish
towards the base, whence a singular kind of horny or
membraneous substance shields the forehead as far as
the eyes: this appendage to the bill is as red as sealing
wax in the breeding season; at other times it varies
or fades into white. The head is small and black, ex-

cept a white spot under each eye; the irides red: all
the upper parts of the plumage dark shining olive
green, inclining to brown: under parts dark hoary
lead grey: vent feathers black; those on the belly and
the thighs tipped with dirty white: the long loose feathers on the sides, which hang over the upper part of
the thighs, are black, streaked with white: the ridge
of the wing, outside feathers of the tail, and those underneath white: upper bare part of the thighs red;
from the knees to the toes, the colours are different
shades, from pale yellow to deep green: toes very
long, the middle one measuring, to the end of the nail,
nearly three inches; their under sides broad, being
furnished with membraneous edgings their whole
length on each side, by which the bird is enabled to
swim, and easily run over the surface of the slimy mud
by the sides of the waters, where it frequents.

The body of the Water Hen is long and compressed
at the sides, and the legs placed far behind; its feathers are thickly set, or compact, and bedded upon
down. Like the Water Rail it lives concealed during
the day, among reeds and willows, by the sides of
rivers or rivulets, which it prefers to bogs and stagnant pools: it can run over the surface of such waters
as are thickly covered with weeds, and it dives and
hides itself with equal ease; it flirts up its tail when
running, and flies with its legs hanging down. In the
evenings, it creeps, runs, and skulks by the margins
of the waters, among the roots of bushes, osiers, and
long loose herbage, in quest of its food, which consists
of water insects, small fishes, worms, aquatic plants
and seeds. It is likewise granivorous: if killed in

September or October, after having had the advantage of a neighbouring stubble, its flesh is very good.

They make their nest of a large quantity of withered reeds and rushes, closely interwoven, and are particularly careful to have it placed in a most retired spot, close by the brink of the water; and it is said, the female never quits it without covering her eggs with the leaves of the surrounding herbage. Pennant and Latham say, she builds upon some low stump of a tree, or shrub, by the water's side: no doubt, she may sometimes vary the place of her nest, according as particular circumstances may command, but she generally prefers the other mode of building it. She lays six or seven eggs at a time, and commonly has two hatchings in a season. The eggs are nearly two inches in length, and are irregularly and thinly marked with rust-coloured spots on a yellowish white ground. The young brood remain but a short time under the nurturing care of the mother; but as soon as they are able to crawl out, they take to the water, and shift for themselves.

Although the Water Hen is no where very numerous, yet one species or other of them is met with in almost every country. It is not yet ascertained whether they ever migrate from this to other countries, but it is well known that they make partial flittings from one district to another, and are found in the cold mountainous tracts in summer, and in lower and warmer situations in winter.

On examination of several specimens of this bird, in full feather, they were found, like most birds of plain plumage, very little different from each other.

THE GREAT-CRESTED GREBE.

GREATER-CRESTED DOUCKER, CARGOOSE, ASH-COLOURED
LOON, OR GAUNT.

(Podiceps cristatus, Lath.—*La Grêbe cornu,* Buff.)

THIS is the largest of the Grebes, weighing about two
pounds and a half, and measuring twenty-one inches in
length, and thirty in breadth. The bill is about two
inches and a quarter long, dark at the tip, and red at
the base: the bare stripe, or lore, between the bill and
the eyes, is in the breeding season red, but afterwards
changes to dusky: irides, fine pale crimson. The head

is furnished with a great quantity of feathers, which form a kind of ruff,* surrounding the upper part of the neck; those on each side of the head, behind, are longer than the rest, and stand out like ears: this ruff is of a bright ferruginous colour, edged on the under side with black. The upper parts of the plumage are of a sooty or mouse-coloured brown; under parts glossy or silvery white; the inner ridge of the wing is white; the secondaries the same, forming an oblique bar across the wings, when closed: the outside of the legs is dusky, the inside and toes pale green.

This species is common in the fens and lakes in various parts of England, where they breed and rear their young. The female conceals her nest among the flags and reeds which grow in the water, upon which it is said to float, and that she hatches her eggs amidst the moisture which oozes through it. It is made of various kinds of dried fibres, stalks and leaves of water plants, and (Pennant says) of the roots of bugbane, stalks of water-lily, pond-weed, and water-violet; when it happens to be blown from among the reeds, it floats about upon the surface of the open water.

These birds are met with in almost every lake in the northern parts of Europe, as far as Iceland, and southward to the Mediterranean; they are also found in various parts of America.

* The greater number of the Grebes, when in full plumage, are provided (without distinction of sex) with feathers forming a crest or ruff.

THE DUSKY GREBE,

BLACK AND WHITE DOBCHICK.

(Podiceps obscurus, Lath.—*Le petit Grêbe*, Buff.)

MEASURES about an inch less in length, and two in
breadth, than the last. The bill is more than an inch
long, pale blue, with reddish edges: lore and orbits
red: irides bright yellow, without that red; upper part
of the head, hinder part of the neck, scapulars, and
rump, dark sooty, or mouse-coloured brown: feathers
on the back nearly of the same colour, but glossy, and
with greyish edges: ridge of the wings and secondary
quills white; the rest of the wing dusky. There is a
pale spot before each eye; cheeks and throat white:
fore part of the neck light brown; and the breast and

belly white and glossy, like satin: thighs and vent covered with dirty white downy feathers: legs white behind, dusky on the outer sides, and pale blue on the inner sides and shins: the toes and webbed membranes are also blue on the upper sides, and dark underneath.

This description was taken from a very perfect bird, caught on Sand Hutton Car, near York, on the 28th of January, 1799, by the Rev. C. Rudston: other specimens of this species have differed in the shades of their plumage and colour of the bill: in some the upper mandible is yellow, from the nostrils to the corners of the mouth, and the under one entirely of that colour.

THE LESSER GUILLEMOT.

MARROT.

(Uria minor, Lath.)

THIS species weighs about nineteen ounces, and measures in length sixteen inches, and in breadth twenty-six. The bill is shaped like that of the last, and is about two inches and a half long: the stroke formed by the divided feathers behind the eye, is dusky, on a white ground: the cheeks, fore part of the neck and the breast, tips of the secondary quills, and the whole of the under parts, are white, except a few dull spots on the auriculars, and some freckles on the breast; the front and crown of the head, back of the neck, and the whole of the upper parts, are dusky, inclining to lead colour: the legs and feet dusky, blushed with red.

Some naturalists suspect that the Lesser Guillemot is only the young of the foregoing species; but this is not yet ascertained, neither is it known where they breed.* They, however, seldom associate with the Guillemots that breed on the British shores, which they visit only during the winter season, and almost all of them retire northward in the spring.

The bird from which the above drawing and description were taken, was caught alive at Tynemouth, in the latter end of September, 1801: the tide had left it in a situation surrounded by rocks, upon the flat sand, from which it could not raise itself to take flight. While the drawing was making, it sat under a table trimming its feathers, and appeared perfectly at ease, and not the least alarmed at the peeping curiosity of the children who surrounded it. When this business was finished, it was taken and set down upon an open part of the shore, where it immediately began to waddle towards the water, with the whole leg and foot extended on the ground; and as soon as it reached its beloved element, it flapped its wings, darted through the surge, dived, and disappeared.

* Montagu says they are a distinct species; that they breed in the arctic regions, and disperse southward in the autumn.

Mr Laurence Edmondston, in his account of the birds of Zetland, says, " this I have the most satisfactory reasons for believing to be the young of the Foolish Guillemot."

THE LESSER IMBER.

A drawing of this bird was presented by G. Strickland, Esq. of Ripon, who adds,—" As this species of the Colymbus much resembles the Imber in the colour of its plumage, I have given it the name of the *Lesser* Imber, as in weight and size it is one-third less. I have not met with any description of it, and the specimen now in my possession is the only one I have seen."

Montagu says these birds vary much in size, and that ours is a young one in its immature plumage. From various intimations, we have little doubt that this, and the bird described in former editions under the name of Imber (C. Immer), are the young of the Great Northern Diver.

THE SANDWICH TERN.

(Sterna Cantiaca, Gm. Linn.)

A pair of these birds, male and female, was shot on the Farn Islands, on the coast of Northumberland, in July, 1802, from the former of which this figure was taken.* They measured two feet nine inches from tip to tip of the wings: the bills were tipped with yellow: the black feathers which capped and adorned their heads were elongated behind, forming a kind of peaked crest, which overhung the nape and hinder part of the neck: the feathers of the fore part of the neck and breast, when ruffled up, appeared delicately and faint-

* These birds, as well as specimens of nearly the whole of the different kinds which breed on the Farn Isles, were, after great trouble and risk, shot there, expressly for the use of this work, by Major Shore and the late Major Henry Forster Gibson, of the 4th dragoons, to whom the author feels deeply indebted for the facilities afforded to the work.

ly blushed with red. In other respects they corresponded so nearly with Mr Latham's accurate description, that to attempt giving any other is needless.—
" Length eighteen inches : bill two inches ; colour black, with the tip horn colour : tongue half the length of the bill : irides hazel : fore-head, crown, hind head, and sides above the eyes black : the rest of the head, neck, under parts of the body and tail, white ; the back and wings pale hoary lead colour : the first five quills hoary black, the inner webs deeply margined with white ; the sixth like the others, but much paler : the rest of the quills like the back : the tail is forked, the outer feathers six inches and a quarter in length ; the wings reach beyond it : legs and claws black : the under part of the feet dusky red." " Some specimens have the top of the head dotted with white." " In young birds the upper parts are much clouded with brown ; and the whole of the top of the head greatly mixed with white : but this is not peculiar, as the young of other Terns with black heads are in the same state." " It is pretty common on the Suffolk and Kentish coasts in the summer months, breeds there in the month of June, is supposed to lay its eggs upon the rocks, and to hatch them about the middle of July." He adds, " Whether these birds only visit us at uncertain seasons, or have hitherto passed unnoticed among other Terns, we know not ; but believe that this has not yet been recorded as a British species." " They generally make their appearance in the neighbourhood of Romney in Kent, about the middle of April, and take their departure in the beginning of September."

THE ROSEATE TERN.

(Sterna Dugalli, Mont.)

MONTAGU mentions this elegant looking bird as an undescribed species of Tern; and from the white feathers of the whole under parts being tinged with a most delicate rosy blush, he has named it as above. The bill is slender, slightly curved, and about an inch and five eighths long; it is jet black excepting at the base, where it is of a bright orange; the irides are black; the head is also black, and the feathers elongated down the back part of the neck; the upper parts pale cinereous; quill feathers narrow, the shafts white, the first has the exterior web black, with a hoary tinge; the others are also hoary next the shafts, and all margined deeply on the inner webs with white to the tips; the tail is greatly forked, extremely slender, and extends two inches beyond the closed wings; the legs and feet, including the bare space of about half an inch above the knees, are of a bright red; the claws black and hooked. The

specimen from which Mr Montagu describes this bird,
was, with several others, shot in the West Highlands of
Scotland, in July, 1812, and presented to him by Dr
McDougall, of Glasgow, who also, in his communications respecting these birds, points out the difference
between them and the other species of Terns, which
swarmed in their company on the same rocky islands.
The above figure was taken from a preserved specimen
of a bird shot on the Farn Isles, in June, 1820, where
several of them, at various times, have been killed.

THE BLACK-BACKED GULL,

GREAT BLACK AND WHITE GULL.

(Larus marinus, Linn.—*Le Goéland noir manteau,*
Buff.*)*

THIS species measures from twenty-six to twenty-
nine inches in length, and five feet nine inches in
breadth, and weighs nearly five pounds. The bill is
pale yellow, very firm, strong, and thick, and nearly
four inches long from the tip to the corners of the
mouth: the projecting angle on the lower mandible is
red, or orange, with a black spot in the middle, on each
side: the irides are yellow, and the edges of the eye-
lids orange. The upper part of the back and wings
black: all the other parts and the tips of the quills are
white: legs pale flesh colour.

The Black-backed Gull is common in the northern parts of Europe, the rocky isles of the North Sea, and in Greenland. Though it was known to Fabricius, it must be very rare in the higher parts of Baffin's Bay, Captain Sabine having seen only one specimen there. They are only thinly scattered on the coasts of England, where they, however, sometimes remain to breed on the highest cliffs which overhang the sea. In their native haunts, their favorite breeding places are high inaccessible islets, covered with long coarse tufty grass. Their eggs are of a round shape, of a dark olive, thinly marked with dusky spots, and quite black at the thicker end. Their cry of *kac, kac, kac,* quickly repeated, is roughly hoarse and disagreeable.*

* A curious habit of this bird is its constantly accompanying flocks of the Shag (Pelecanus Graculus) at those times of the day when they resort to their favorite rocks to rest themselves, or bask in the sun. Before the sportsman can approach within gunshot, their friendly sentinel, the Black-backed Gull, flies off, and with him all the Shags, excepting a few of the more stupid or very young birds, which not benefiting by the signal, generally fall a sacrifice. (Vide Dr Edmondston's View of the Zetland Islands.)

THE DUN-DIVER,

SPARLING FOWL, OR FEMALE GOOSANDER.

(Mergus Castor, Linn.—*Le Harle cendré, ou le Bievre*,
Buff.)

THE bill, from the tip to the corners of the mouth,
is two inches and a quarter long, of a red colour, but
darker on its ridge; the hooked horny nail of the upper mandible is blackish; the tip of the under one
white: the head and upper part of the neck deep chesnut; the crest, the feathers of which are soft, very long,
and pendent, is of a deeper shade of the same colour:
the chin and upper part of the throat are white: the
back, scapulars, coverts of the wings, rump, and sides
of the body, are of a bluish ash or lead colour: the
fore part of the neck, the breast, belly, and vent, are
yellowish white; the bastard and primary quills dark
brown: a large white patch or bar is formed on the

middle of the wing, by the tips of the greater coverts and the outer webs of six of the secondary quills; but those nearest to the body are of a hoary dark ash: the tail, which consists of fourteen feathers, is nearly of the same colour: the legs orange red.

We have hitherto expressed ourselves doubtfully as to this bird being the female Goosander, seeing that all our contemporaries were at variance on the subject. Dr Heysham, of Carlisle, was probably the first who, by dissection, removed some of the doubts in which this matter was involved: in his Catalogue of Cumberland Animals,* he says, " This has generally been considered as the female of the Goosander." " The following circumstances which have come under my observation, however, render this opinion somewhat doubtful: 1st, The Dun-divers are far more numerous than the Goosanders. 2nd, The Dun-divers are all less than the Goosanders, (the largest I have seen being little more than three pounds) but of various sizes, some being under two pounds. 3rd, The crest of the Dun-diver is considerably longer than the crest (if it can be so called) of the Goosander. 4th, Dun-divers have been found, upon dissection, to be males. 5th, The neck of the largest Dun-diver, and which has proved to be a male, is nothing like so thick as the neck of the Goosander." " On the 26th of December, 1783, I dissected a Dun-diver, which was rather more than three pounds in weight; its length was twenty-seven inches, and its breadth thirty-five inches. It

* See the additional ornaments to Hutchinson's History of Cumberland.

proved to be a male: the testes, though flaccid, were very distinct, and about half an inch in length. In the middle of January, 1786, I received two Dun-divers, both of which I dissected: the first was a small one, about two pounds in weight; it proved to be a female; the eggs were very distinct: the second was much larger, and weighed three pounds; its crest was longer, and its belly of a fine yellowish rose colour: it was a male, and the testes were beginning to grow turgid. I have dissected only one Goosander, and that proved to be a male. Therefore, until a Goosander be found, upon dissection, to prove a female, or two Goosanders to attend the same nest, the doubts respecting these birds cannot be satisfactorily removed."

Although Willoughly describes this as the female Goosander, yet he expresses his doubts of the matter, from its being, like that bird, furnished with a kind of large labyrinth, which, he says, is to be found in the males only of the Duck tribe, and whence he conjectures that this is also peculiar to all the males of the *Mergi*, and that all the females are without it; but he notices one of this family (which at Venice is called *Cokall*) in which this labyrinth, or enlargement of the windpipe, was wanting. Respecting the Dun-diver he further observes, that " the stomach of this bird is as it were a craw and a gizzard joined together. The upper part, resembling the craw, hath no wrinkles or folds in its inner membrane, but is only granulated with small papillary glandules, resembling the little protuberances on the third ventricle of a Beef, called the Manifold, or those on the shell of a Sea-urchin."

These discrepancies have, we think, been satisfacto-

rily accounted for by Temminck, who informs us that
" the young males of the first year appear in the livery
of their mothers :" this is doubtless the reason why Dr
Heysham failed in actually reaching the truth, while
he approached so very near to it by the only infallible
route, dissection. The same able naturalist (Temminck) has furnished us with facilities of discrimina-
ting the females and young males of this species from
those of the Red-breasted Merganser, points which
have hitherto created very great difficulty. He says
" the females and the young males of the Goosander
are distinguished by their greater size, but especially
by the white spot on the wings, which in them is of an
uniform colour, while in the Red-breasted Merganser,
it is transversely barred with ash in the females, and
blackish in the young males."

The above figure was drawn from one in full plumage and perfection, for which this work was indebted to Robert Pearson, Esq. of Newcastle, the 28th of
February, 1801.

THE RED-BREASTED MERGANSER.

(Mergus Serrator, Linn.—*Le Harle huppè,* Buff.)

THIS bird measures one foot nine inches in length,
and two feet seven in breadth, and weighs about two
pounds. The bill, from the tip to the angles of the
mouth, is three inches in length, slender, and of a rather roundish form, and like those of the rest of this
genus, hooked at the tip, and toothed on the edges:
the upper mandible is dark brown, tinged with green,
and edged with red; the lower one wholly red; the
irides are deep red: the head, long pendent crest, and
upper part of the neck, are of a glossy violet black,
changing in different lights to a beautiful gilded green:
the rest of the neck and belly white: the breast rusty
red, spotted with black on the front, and bordered on
each side with five or six white feathers, edged with

black : the upper part of the back, glossy black; the lower, the rump, and sides, are prettily marked with transverse zigzag lines of brown and pale grey : the ridge of the wings, and adjoining coverts are dusky; the feathers nearest to the wings are white : the greater coverts, and some of the secondary quills, black and white; the others, and the scapulars, are also party-coloured of the same hue : the primary quills are black; some of those next to the body tipped with white, and others of them white on the upper half, and black to their points; the white spot on the wing barred in the male by two black lines. The tail is short, its colour brown : the legs and feet of a deep saffron red. These birds, both male and female, are said to differ much in their plumage; some having more white on them than others, and some also brighter colours, and more distinctly marked.

The female (which the author has not seen) is described as differing from the male in having only the rudiment of a crest, and in the white spot of the wing being crossed by only one transverse bar. Pennant says—" The head and upper part of the neck are of a deep rust colour: throat white: fore part of the neck and breast marbled with deep ash colour : belly white: great quill feathers dusky : lower half of the nearest secondaries black; the upper white : the rest dusky : back, scapulars, and tail, ash coloured : the upper half of the secondary feathers white; the lower half black; the others dusky."

In a male of this species which was shot at Sandwich, in Kent, Latham says—" I observed that the feathers which compose the crest, were simply black;

also down the middle of the crown, as well as the space before the eye, and beneath the chin and throat; but in the rest of the neck the black had a gloss of green." He also describes it as having " a curious and large labyrinth," similar to those of other males of this genus, which have been noticed before.

The Red-breasted Merganser is not common in Britain, particularly in the southern parts of the island; but they are met with in great flocks at Newfoundland, Greenland, and Hudson's Bay, during the summer months; they are found also in various other northern parts of the world, and in the Mediterranean sea.

THE SMEW.

WHITE NUN.

(Mergus albellus, Linn.—*Le petit Harle huppé, ou la Piette*, Buff.)

THE Smew is about the size of a Wigeon: the bill is
nearly two inches long, of a dusky blue, thickest at the
base, and tapering into a more slender and narrow shape
towards the point: it is toothed like those of the rest of
this tribe: the irides are dark: on each side of the head,
an oval-shaped black patch, glossed with green, is extended from the corners of the mouth over the eyes:
under side of the crest black; the other parts of the
head and neck white: the breast, belly, and vent are
also white, excepting a curved black stroke, pointing
forward from the shoulders on each side of the upper

part of the breast, which, on the lower part, has also similar strokes pointing the same way: the back, the coverts on the ridge of the wings, and the primary quills are black: the secondaries and greater coverts black, tipped with white: the middle coverts and the scapulars white: the sides, under the wings to the tail, are agreeably variegated and crossed with dark waved lines. The tail consists of sixteen dark ash coloured feathers; the middle ones about three inches and a half long, the rest gradually tapering off shorter on each side: the legs and feet are of a bluish lead colour. This species, which seldom visits this country except in very severe winters, is at once distinguished from the rest of the *Mergi* by its black and white piebald appearance, although the individuals vary from each other in the proportion and extent of those colours on their plumage.

The Red-headed Smew had long been considered by some ornithologists as a distinct species; while others have maintained that it is the female of the Smew. It is now, however, ascertained to be the immature male of that bird.

THE MUTE SWAN.

TAME SWAN.

(Anas Olor, Linn.—*Le Cygne,* Buff.)

THE plumage of this species is of the same snowy
whiteness as that of the Wild Swan, and the bird is
covered next the body with the same kind of fine close
down; but it greatly exceeds the Wild Swan in size,
weighing about twenty-five pounds, and measuring
more in the length of the body and extent of the wings.
This also differs in being furnished with a projecting,
callous, black tubercle, or knob on the base of the up-

per mandible, and in the colour of the bill, which is red, with black edges and tip: the naked skin between the bill and the eyes is also of the latter colour: in the Wild Swan this bare space is yellow. There is nothing peculiar in the structure of the windpipe, which enters the lungs in a straight line.

The manners and habits are much the same in both kinds, particularly when they are in a wild state; for indeed this species cannot properly be called domesticated; they are only as it were partly reclaimed from a state of nature, and invited by the friendly and protecting hand of man to decorate and embellish the artificial lakes and pools which beautify his pleasure grounds. On these the Swan cannot be accounted a captive, for he enjoys all the sweets of liberty. Placed there, as he is the largest of all the British birds, so is he to the eye the most pleasing and elegant. What in nature can be more beautiful than the grassy-margined lake, hung round with the varied foliage of the grove, when contrasted with the pure resplendent whiteness of the majestic Swan, wafted along with erected plumes, by the gentle breeze, or floating, reflected on the glossy surface of the water, while he throws himself into numberless graceful attitudes, as if desirous of attracting the admiration of the spectator !

The Swan, although possessed of the power to rule, yet molests none of the other water birds, and is singularly social and attentive to those of his own family, which he protects from every insult. While they are employed with the cares of the young brood, it is not safe to approach near them, for they will fly upon any stranger, whom they often beat to the ground by re-

peated blows; and they have been known by a stroke
of the wing to break a man's leg. But, however powerful they are with their wings, yet a slight blow on the
head will kill them.

The Swan, for ages past, has been protected on the
river Thames as royal property; and it continues at
this day to be accounted felony to steal their eggs.
" By this means their increase is secured, and they
prove a delightful ornament to that noble river." Latham says, " In the reign of Edward IV. the estimation they were held in was such, that no one who possessed a freehold of less than the clear yearly value of
five marks, was permitted even to keep any." In those
times, hardly a piece of water was left unoccupied by
these birds, as well on account of the gratification they
gave to the eye of their lordly owners, as that which
they also afforded when they graced the sumptuous
board at the splendid feasts of that period: but the
fashion of those days is passed away, and Swans are
not nearly so common now as they were formerly, being by most people accounted a coarse kind of food,
and consequently held in little estimation: but the
Cygnets (so the young Swans are called) are still fattened for the table, and are sold very high, commonly
for a guinea each, and sometimes for more: hence it
may be presumed they are better food than is generally imagined.

This species is said to be found in great numbers in
Russia and Siberia, as well as further southward, in a
wild state. They are, without an owner, common on
the river Trent, and on the salt-water inlet of the sea,
near Abbotsbury, in Dorsetshire: they are also met

with on other rivers and lakes in different parts of the British isles.

It is the generally received opinion that the Swan lives to a very great age, some say a century, and others have protracted their lives to three hundred years! Strange as this may appear, there are who credit it: the author, however, does not scruple to hazard an opinion, that this over-stretched longevity originates only in traditionary tales, or in idle unfounded hearsay stories; as no one has yet been able to say, with certainty, to what age they attain.

The female makes her nest, concealed among the rough herbage, near the water's edge: she lays from six to eight large white eggs, and sits on them about six weeks (some say eight weeks) before they are hatched. The young do not acquire their full plumage till the second year.

It is found by experience that the Swan will not thrive if kept out of the water: confined in a court yard, he makes an awkward figure, and soon becomes dirty, tawdry, dull, and spiritless.

THE SWAN GOOSE,

CHINESE, SPANISH, GUINEA, OR CAPE GOOSE.

(Anas Cygnoides, Linn.—*L'Oie de Guinée,* Buff.)

Is more than three feet in length, and of a size between the Swan and the Common Goose: it is distinguished from others of the Goose tribe by its up-
right and stately deportment, by having a large knob
on the base of the upper mandible, and a skin, almost
bare of feathers, hanging down like a pouch, or a wattle, under the throat:* a white line or fillet is extended from the corners of the mouth over the front of the
brow: the base of the bill is orange: irides reddish

* The bird from which the above figure was taken, was without
this appendage.

brown: a dark brown or black stripe runs down the
hinder part of the neck, from the head to the back:
the fore part of the neck, and the breast, are yellowish
brown: the back, and all the upper parts, brownish
grey, edged with a lighter colour: the sides, and the
feathers which cover the thighs, are clouded nearly of
the same colours as the back, and edged with white:
belly white: legs orange.

It is said that these birds originally were found in
Guinea only: now they are become pretty common, in
a wild as well as a domesticated state, both in warm
and in cold climates.

Tame Geese of this species, like other kinds, vary
much, both in the colour of the bill, legs, and plumage,
as well as in size; but they all retain the knob on the
base of the upper mandible, and rarely want the pouch
or wattle under the gullet. They are kept by the curious in various parts of England, and are more noisy
than the common Goose: nothing can stir, in the night
or day, without their sounding the alarm, by their
hoarse cacklings and shrill cries. They breed with the
Common Goose, and their offspring are as prolific as
those of any other kind. The female is smaller than
the male: " the head, neck, and breast are fulvous;
paler on the upper part: the back, wings, and tail,
dull brown, with pale edges: belly white: in other respects they are like the male, but the knob over the
bill is smaller."

THE TAME GOOSE.

(Anas Anser, Linn.—*L'Oie domestique,* Buff.)

To describe the varied plumage and the economy of
this well-known valuable domestic fowl, may seem to
many a needless task; but to others, unacquainted
with rural affairs, it may be interesting.* Their predominant colours are white and grey, with shades of
ash, blue, and brown: some of them are yellowish,
others dusky, and many are found to differ very little
in appearance from the wild kind before described—the
original stock whence, in early times, they were all
derived. The only permanent mark, which all the
grey ones still retain, like those of the wild kind, is
the white ring which surrounds the root of the .tail.

* A certain town lady wondered how a Goose could suckle nine
Goslings.

They are generally furnished with a small tuft on the head; and the most usual colour of the males (Gander or Steg) is pure white: the bills and feet in both males and females are of an orange red. By studied attention in the breeding, two sorts of these Geese have been obtained: the less are by many esteemed as being more delicate eating; the larger are by others preferred on account of the bountiful appearance they make upon the festive board. The weight of the latter kind is generally between nine and fifteen pounds; but instances are not wanting, where they have been fed to upwards of twenty pounds: this is, however, to sacrifice the flavour of the food to the size and appearance of the bird; for they become disgustingly fat and surfeiting, and the methods used to cram them up are unnatural and cruel. It is not, however, altogether on account of their use as food that they are valuable; their feathers, their down, and their quills,* have long been considered as articles of more importance, and from which their owners reap more advantages. In this respect the poor creatures have not been spared: urged by avarice, their inhuman masters appear to have ascertained the exact quantity of plumage of which they can bear to be robbed, without being deprived of life. Mr

* " An English archer bent his bow,
  " Made of a trusty tree,—
" An arrow of a cloth yard long,
  " Unto the head drew he:

" Against Sir Hugh Montgomery
  " So right his shaft he set,
" The grey Goosewing that was thereon
  " In his heart's blood was wet."

Chevy Chace.

Pennant, in describing the methods used in Lincolnshire, in breeding, rearing, and plucking Geese, says,
" they are plucked five times in the year: first at Lady-
day for the feathers and quills; this business is renew-
ed for the feathers only, four times more between that
and Michaelmas:" he adds, that he saw the operation
performed even upon Goslings of six weeks old, from
which the feathers of the tails were plucked; and that
numbers of the Geese die when the season afterwards
proves cold.   But this unfeeling greedy business is not
peculiar to one county, for much the same is practised
in others.   The care and attention bestowed upon the
brood Geese, while they are engaged in the business
of incubation, in the month of April, is nearly the
same every where: wicker pens are provided for them,
placed in rows, and tier above tier, not uncommonly
under the same roof with their owner.   Some place
water and corn near the nests; others drive them to
the water twice a-day, and replace each female upon
her own nest as soon as she returns.   This business
requires the attendance of the Gozzard (Goose-herd) a
month at least, in which time the young are brought
forth: as soon afterwards as the brood are able to waddle along, they are, together with their dams, driven to
the contiguous loughs, and fens or marshes, on whose
grassy-margined pools they feed and thrive, without
requiring any further attendance until the autumn.   To
these marshes, which otherwise would be unoccupied,
(except by wild birds) and be only useless watery
wastes, we are principally indebted for so great a supply of the Goose; for in almost every country where
lakes and marshes abound, the neighbouring inhabi-

tants keep as many as suit their convenience, and in this way immense numbers annually attain to full growth and perfection. But in no part of the world are such numbers reared as in the fens of Lincolnshire, where it is said to be no uncommon thing for a single person to keep a thousand old Geese, each of which, on an average, will bring up seven young ones. So far those only are noticed which may properly be called the larger flocks, by which particular watery districts are peopled; and, although their aggregate numbers are great, yet they form only a part of the large family: those of the farm-yard, taken separately, appear as small specks, on a great map; but when they are gathered together, and added to those kept by almost every cottager throughout the kingdom, the immense whole will appear multiplied in a ratio almost incalculable. A great part of those which are left to provide for themselves during the summer, in the solitary distant waters, as well as those which enliven the village green, are put into the stubble fields after harvest, to fatten upon the scattered grain; and some are penned up for this purpose, by which they attain to greater bulk; and it is hardly necessary to observe, that they are then poured in weekly upon the tables of the luxurious citizens of every town in the kingdom. But these distant and divided supplies seem trifling when compared with the multitudes which, in the season, are driven in all directions into the metropolis:* the former appear only like the scanty waterings of the petty streamlet; the latter like the copious overflowing

* In ancient times they were driven in much the same way, from the interior of Gaul to Rome.

torrent of a large river. To the country market towns
they are carried in bags and panniers; to the great
centre of trade they are sent in droves of many thousands.* To a stranger it is a most curious spectacle
to view these hissing, cackling, gabbling, but peaceful
armies, with grave deportment, waddling along (like
other armies) to certain destruction. The drivers are
each provided with a long stick, at one end of which a
red rag is tied as a lash, and a hook is fixed at the
other: with the former, of which the Geese seem much
afraid, they are excited forward; and with the latter,
such as attempt to stray, are caught by the neck and
kept in order; or if lame, they are put into an *hospital
cart*, which usually follows each large drove. In this
manner they perform their journies from distant parts,
and are said to get forward at the rate of eight or ten
miles in a day, from three in the morning till nine at
night: those which become fatigued are fed with oats,
and the rest with barley.

It is universally believed that the Goose lives to a
great age, and particular instances are recorded by
ornithologists, which confirm the fact: some are mentioned which have been kept seventy years; and Willoughby notices one which lived eighty years. They
are, however, seldom permitted to live out their natural life, being sold with the younger ones long before
they approach that period. The old ones are called
cagmags, and are bought only by novices in market-

---

* In an article which Mr Latham has copied from the St James's
Chronicle of September 2nd, 1783, it is noticed, that a drove of about
nine thousand Geese passed through Chelmsford on their way to London, from Suffolk.

making; for, from their toughness, they are utterly unfit for the table.

The Tame Goose lays from seven to twelve eggs, and sometimes more: these the careful housewife divides equally among her brood Geese, when they begin to sit. Those which lay a second time in the course of the summer, are seldom, if ever, permitted to have a second hatching; but the eggs are used for household purposes. In some countries the domestic Geese require much less care and attendance than those of this country. Buffon, in his elegant and voluminous Ornithology, in which nothing is omitted, gives a particular detail of their history and economy every where: he informs us, that among the villages of the Cossacks, subject to Russia, on the river Don, the Geese leave their homes, in March or April, as soon as the ice breaks up, and the pairs joining each other, take flight in a body to the remote northern lakes, where they breed and constantly reside during the summer; and that on the beginning of winter, the parent birds, with their multiplied young progeny, all return, and divide themselves, every flock alighting at the door of the respective place to which it belongs.

The Goose has for many ages been celebrated on account of its vigilance. The story of their saving Rome by the alarm they gave, when the Gauls were attempting the capitol,* is well known, and was probably the first time of their watchfulness being recorded; and on that account, they were afterwards held in the

---

* As the poet sings—
" Et servaturis vigili Capitolia voce Anseribus."

highest estimation by the Roman people. It is certain, that nothing can stir in the night, nor the least or most distant noise be made, but the Geese are roused, and immediately begin to hold their cackling converse; and on the nearer approach of apprehended danger, they set up their more shrill and clamorous cries. It is on account of this property that they are esteemed by many persons, as the most vigilant of all sentinels, when placed in particular situations.

THE WHITE-FRONTED WILD GOOSE,

LAUGHING GOOSE.

(Anas albifrons.—L'Oie rieuse, Buff.)

MEASURES two feet four inches in length, and four feet six in the extended wings, and weighs about five pounds. Bill thick at the base, of a yellowish red; nail white; from the base of the bill and corners of the mouth, a white patch is extended over the forehead: rest of the head, neck, and the upper parts of the plumage in some specimens are dark brown, in others they vary to a lighter brown, and each feather is margined more or less with that colour: the primary and secondary quills are of the same, but much darker; and the wing coverts are tinged with ash: breast and belly dirty white, and barred with irregular patches of very dark brown, tipped with lighter shades of that colour:

the tail hoary ash-coloured brown, and surrounded with
a white ring at the base : the legs yellow.

These birds form a part of those vast tribes which
swarm about Hudson's Bay, and the north of Europe
and Asia, during the summer months, and are but
thinly scattered over the other quarters of the world.
They visit the fens and marshy places in England, in
small flocks, in the winter months, and disappear about
the beginning of March.   It is said that they never feed
on the corn fields, but confine themselves wholly to
such wilds and swamps as are constantly covered with
water.

THE EIDER DUCK.

ST CUTHBERT'S DUCK.

(*Anas mollissima*, Linn.—*L'Eider*, Buff.)

THIS wild, but valuable, species is of a size between
the Goose and the Domestic Duck, and appears to be
one of the graduated links of the chain which connects
the two kinds.   The full-grown old males generally
measure about two feet two inches in length, and two
feet eighteen in breadth, and weigh from six to above
seven pounds.   The head is large; the middle of the
neck small, with the lower part of it spread out very
broad, so as to form a hollow between the shoulders,
which, while the bird is sitting at ease, seems as if fitted to receive its reclining head.   The bill is of a dirty
yellowish horn colour, darkish in the middle, and measures, from the tip to the corners of the mouth, two
inches and a half: the upper mandible is forked in a

singular manner towards each eye, and is covered with
white feathers on the sides, as far forward as the nostrils.
The upper part of the head is of a soft velvet black,
divided behind by a dull white stroke pointing downwards: the feathers from the nape of the neck to the
throat, are long, or puffed out, overhanging the upper
part of the neck, and look as if they had been clipped
off at the lower ends: they have the appearance of a
pale pea-green velvet shag, with a white line dropping
downward from the auriculars on each side. The
cheeks, chin, upper part of the neck, the back, and
lesser wing coverts, are white: the scapulars, and secondary quills, next the body, dirty white: bastard
wings, and primary quills brown; secondaries and
greater coverts the same, but much darker: the lower
broad part of the neck, on the front, to the breast, is
of a buff colour; but in some specimens tinged with
rusty red: the breast, belly, vent, rump, and tail coverts are of a deep sooty black: tail feathers hoary
brown: legs short, and yellow: webs and nails dusky.
The female is nearly of the same shape, though less
than the male, weighing only between five and six
pounds; but her plumage is quite different, the ground
colour being of a reddish brown, prettily crossed with
waved black lines; and in some specimens the neck,
breast, and belly, are tinged with ash: the wings are
crossed with two bars of white: quills dark: the neck
is marked with longitudinal dusky streaks, and the
belly is deep brown, spotted obscurely with black.

The Eider Duck lays from three to five large,
smooth, pale olive-coloured eggs; these she deposits
and conceals in a nest, or bed, made of a great quan-

tity of the soft, warm, elastic down, plucked from her own breast, and sometimes from that of her mate. The ground work or foundation of the nest is formed of bent-grass, sea-weeds, or such like coarse materials, and it is placed in as sheltered a spot as the bleak and solitary place can afford.

In Greenland, Iceland, Spitzbergen, Lapland, and some parts of the coasts of Norway, the Eiders flock together, in particular breeding places, in such numbers, and their nests are so close together, that a person in walking along can hardly avoid treading upon them. The natives of these cold climates eagerly watch the time when the first hatchings of the eggs are laid: of these they rob the nest, and also of the more important article, the down with which it is lined, which they carefully gather and carry off. These birds will afterwards strip themselves of their remaining down, and lay a second hatching, of which also they are sometimes robbed: but it is said, that when this cruel treatment is too often repeated, they leave the place and return to it no more.*   The quantity of this valu-

* The following particulars, from Von Troil's Letters on Iceland, are given on account of the singular trait of character which is mentioned—that of two females occupying only one nest :—

" The Eider birds build their nest on little islands not far from the shore, and sometimes even near the dwellings of the natives, who treat them with such kindness and circumspection as to make them quite tame.   In the beginning of June they lay five or six eggs, and it is not unusual to find from ten to sixteen eggs in one nest, with two females, who agree remarkably well together.   The whole time of laying continues six or seven weeks, during which time the natives visit the nest for the purpose of taking the down and eggs, at least once a week.   They first carefully remove the female, and then take away the down and part of the eggs ; after which she lays afresh, co-

able commodity, which is thus annually collected in various parts is uncertain. Buffon mentions one particular year, in which the Icelandic company sold as much as amounted to upwards of eight hundred and fifty pounds sterling. This, however, must be only a small portion of the produce, which is all sold by the hardy natives, to stuff the couches of the pampered citizens of more polished nations.

The great body of these birds constantly resides in the remote northern, frozen climates, the rigours of which their thick cloathing well enables them to bear. They are said to keep together in flocks in the open parts of the sea, diving very deep in quest of shell-fish and other food, with which the bottom is covered; and when they have satisfied themselves, they retire to the shore, whither they at all times repair for shelter, on the approach of a storm. Other less numerous flocks of the Eiders branch out, colonize, and breed further southward in both Europe and America: they are found on the promontories and numerous isles of the

vering her eggs with new down plucked from her breast : this being taken away, the male comes to her assistance, and covers the eggs with his down, which is left till the young are hatched. One female, during the whole time of laying, generally gives half a pound of down. The down from dead birds is accounted of little worth, having lost its elasticity. There are generally exported fifteen hundred or two thousand pounds of down on the company's account, exclusive of what is privately sold. The young ones quit the nest soon after they are hatched, and follow the female, who leads them to the water, where, having taken them on her back, she swims with them a few yards, and then dives, and leaves them floating on the water: in this situation they soon learn to take care of themselves, and are seldom afterwards seen on the land, but live among the rocks, and feed on insects and sea-weed."

coast of Norway, and on those of the Northern and
Western islands of Scotland, and also on the Farn
Isles, on the Northumberland coast, which latter is the
only place where they are known to breed in England,
and may be said to be their utmost southern limit in
this quarter, although a few solitary instances of single
birds being shot further southward along the coast have
sometimes happened. Mr Tunstall had a stuffed specimen in his museum, which was shot in January, at
Hartlepool, on the Durham coast. The foregoing
figure and description were taken from a perfect bird,
in full plumage, shot in April, near Holy Island.

It is not known that any attempts to domesticate this
species have succeeded. Such as were made by the
late Rev. Dr Thorp, of Ryton, entirely failed of success.

THE MUSK DUCK.

CAIRO, GUINEA, OR INDIAN DUCK.

(Anas moschata, Linn.—*Le Canard Musque,* Buff.)

THIS species is much larger than the Common Duck, measuring about two feet feet in length. The irides are pale yellow; the bill from the tip to the protuberance on the brow, is more than two inches long. Domestication, from time to time, has made a great variation in the plumage of these birds, but they are all alike in having a fleshy knob on the base of the bill, and a naked, red, warty or carunculated skin extending from that and the chin to above the eyes, and in having the crown of the head rather tufted and black, which they can erect at pleasure. The legs are short and thick, and as well as the toes, vary in different birds from red to yellow.

Ornithologists are in doubt as to the country to which these birds originally belonged; it is, however, agreed, that they are natives of the warm climates. Pennant says they are met with, wild, about the lake Baikal, in Asia; Ray, that they are natives of Louisiana; Marcgrave, that they are met with in Brazil; and Buffon, that they are found in the overflowed savannas of Guiana, where they feed in the day-time upon the wild rice, and return in the evening to the sea; he adds, " they nestle on the trunks of rotten trees; and after the young are hatched, the mother takes them one after another by the bill and throws them into the water." It is said that great numbers of the young brood are destroyed by the alligators, which are common in those parts.

These birds have obtained the name of Musk Duck, from their musky smell, which arises from the liquor secreted in the glands on the rump. They breed readily with the Common Duck, forming an intermediate kind, better suited to the table than either of the parents. The Hybrids do not appear to be productive.

In former editions of this work, the description of the plumage of these birds was taken from other ornithologists, whose accuracy cannot be doubted. The bill red, except about the nostrils and tip, where it is brown; the cheeks, throat, and fore part of the neck, white, irregularly marked with black : the belly, from the breast to the thighs, white. The general colour of the rest of the plumage is deep brown, darkest

and glossed with green, on the back, rump, quills, and
tail; the two outside feathers of the latter, and the first
three of the quills, are white.

The above is the general appearance of the Musk
Duck; but the living specimen from which our figure
was drawn, was, excepting the head, entirely white.
The bird was lent to this work by William Losh, Esq.
of Point Pleasant, near Newcastle, who has had a
breed of them for several years. The original pair
came from France: they were white, and their progeny continue the same. They are completely domesticated, are disposed to perch on trees and out-houses,
but the smallest disturbance will cause them to abandon their nest. They are easily reared, producing at
a hatching eight, ten, or twelve, according to the care
bestowed upon them.

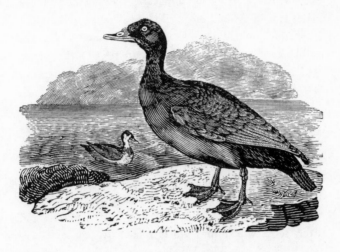

THE SCOTER,

BLACK DUCK, OR BLACK DIVER.

(Anas nigra, Linn.—*La Macreuse,* Buff.)

WEIGHS generally about two pounds nine ounces, and measures sixteen or eighteen inches in length, and thirty-four in breadth. The base of the upper mandible is raised up into a kind of large knob, divided downwards in the middle by a narrow bright or deep yellow stripe, which is spread round the projecting edges of the nostrils, and extended nearly to the tip: the rest of the bill is black, grooved along near the edges, where it is broad and flat: the under mandible is also black: irides dusky. From the curious conformation and appearance of the bill, (of which a more accurate figure is subjoined) this species cannot easily be mistaken, although it is said that the knob in some specimens is red: in that

of the females it is hardly noticeable; and in the younger
males it is of a small size.   The eyelids are yellow, the
irides dark, and the whole of its close smooth plumage
is black, glossed on the head and neck with purple.
The tail consists of sixteen sharp-pointed feathers, of
which the middle are the longest: legs brown.   In
some of the young females the plumage is grey.

In seveie winters the Scoters leave the northern extremities of the world in immense flocks, dispersing
themselves southward along the shores of more temperate climates.   They are only sparingly scattered on
the coasts of England; but according to Buffon, they
appear in great numbers upon the northern coasts of
France, to which they are attracted by beds of a certain kind of small bivalve shell-fish, *(vaimeaux)* which
abound in those parts, and of which they are very fond,
for they are almost incessantly diving in quest of them.
Over these beds of shell-fish, the fishermen at low water
spread their long nets, floated or supported horizontally
two or three feet from the sand : these they leave to be
covered by the overflowing tide, which also brings the
Scoters prowling along with it, within their accustomed distance from the beach.   As soon as the first of
them perceives the shells, it instantly dives, when all
the rest follow the example, and numbers are entangled
in the floating meshes of the net.   In this way it is said
that sometimes twenty or thirty dozen have been taken
in a single tide.   These birds are sold to the Roman
Catholics, who eat them on fast days and in Lent, when
their religious ordinances have forbidden the use of all
animal food except fish; but these birds, and a few
others of the same fishy flavour, have been exempted

from the interdict, on the supposition of their being
cold-blooded, and partaking of the nature of fish.

The Scoters seldom quit the sea, upon which they
are very nimble, and are indefatigable expert divers;
but they fly heavily, near the surface of the water, and
to no great distance, and are said to walk awkwardly
erect on the land.

THE TAME DUCK.

(Anas domestica, Linn.—*Le Canard domestique,* Buff.)

THIS valuable domestic owes its origin to the Mallard, the last described species, but has long been reclaimed from a state of nature. Many of them appear in nearly the same plumage as the wild ones; others vary greatly from them, as well as from each other, and may be said to be marked with almost all colours; but all the males (Drakes) still retain the unvarying mark of their wild original, in the curled feathers of the tail. Long domestication has, however, deprived the Tame Duck of that keen, quick, and sprightly look and shape which distinguish the Mallard, and substituted a more dull and less elegant form and appearance in their stead. In the wild state they pair, and are monogamous, but become polygamous when tame.

The Count de Buffon, whose lively and ingenious

flights of imagination are peculiar to himself, says
" Man made a double conquest when he subdued inhabitants at once of the air and of the water. Free in
both these vast elements, equally fitted to roam in the
regions of the atmosphere, to glide through the ocean
or plunge under its billows, the aquatic birds seemed
destined by nature to live for ever remote from our society, and from the limits of our dominion." " Eggs
taken from the reeds and rushes amidst the water, and
set under an adopted mother, first produced, in our
farm-yards, wild, shy, fugitive birds, perpetually roving
and unsettled, and impatient to regain the abodes of liberty." These, however, after they had bred and reared their own young in the domestic asylum, became attached to the spot; and their descendants in process of
time, grew more and more gentle and tractable, till at
last they appear to have nearly relinquished and for-
gotten the prerogatives of the savage state, although
they still retain a strong propensity to roam abroad, in
search, no doubt, of the larger pools, marshy places,
and bogs, which it is natural to suppose they must prefer to the beaten, hard, pebbly-covered surface, surrounding the scantily watered hamlet: and indeed it is
well known to every observing good housewife, that
where they are long confined to such dry places, they
degenerate in both strength and beauty, and lose much
of the fine flavour of those which are reared in spots
more congenial to their nature. That these, and such
like watery places, which their health requires for them
to wash, dive, feed, rest, and sport in, are not better
tenanted by these useful and pretty birds, is much to
be regretted, and marks strongly a falling off—a want

of industry* in those females to whose lot it falls, and
whose duty it is to contribute their quota of attention
to these lesser but not uninteresting branches of rural
economy.   Were this done, and ponds made in aid of
the purpose, in every suitable contiguous situation,
there can be no doubt but that a multiplied stock of
Ducklings, to an inconceivable amount, might be annually reared, with a comparatively trifling additional
expence; for the various undistinguishable animal and
vegetable substances upon which they chiefly live, and
for which they unceasingly search with their curiously
constructed bills, sifting and separating every alimenta-
ry particle from the mud, unless fed upon by them, are
totally lost.   When older, they also devour worms,
spawn, water insects, and sometimes frogs and small
fishes, together with the various seeds of bog and water
plants, of which they find an abundant supply when left
to provide for themselves in those wet places.

When they, with other kinds of fowl, are busily employed in picking up the waste about the barn door,
they greatly enliven and beautify the rural scene.

    " A snug thack house, before the door a green ;
    " Hens on the midding, ducks in dubs are seen :
    " On this side stands a barn, on that a byre ;
    " A peat-stack joins, and forms a rural square."†

To this may be added the no less pleasing peep at the
mill and mill-dam, when well furnished with these their
feathered inhabitants.   The village school-boy witness-

---

   * " The thrifty huswife is aye weel kend by her sonsy swarms
o'bonny chucky burdies."   *Scotch Proverb.*
                † Allan Ramsay.

es with delight the antic movements of the busy shape-
less little brood, sometimes under the charge of a foster
mother, who with anxious fears paddles by the brink,
and utters her unavailing cries, while the Ducklings, regardless of her warnings, and rejoicing in the element
so well adapted to their nature, are splashing over each
other beneath the pendent foliage; or, in eager pursuit,
snap at their insect prey on the surface, or plunge after
them to the bottom: some meanwhile are seen perpendicularly suspended, with the tail only above water, engaged in the general search after food.

Scenes like these, harmonized by the clack of the
mill and its murmuring water-fall, afford pleasures little
known to those who have always been engaged in mere
worldly pursuits: but such picturesque beauties pass
not unnoticed by the young naturalist; their charms
invite his first attentions, and probably bias his inclinations to pursue studies which enlarge and exalt his
mind, and can only end with his life.

THE GADWALL.

(Anas strepera, Linn.—*Le Chipeau,* Buff.)

THE Gadwall measures about nineteen inches in length, and twenty-three in breadth. The bill is flat, black, and two inches long, from the tip to the corners of the mouth : the head, and upper part of the neck, are of a rufous brown colour, lightest on the throat and cheeks, and finely speckled and dotted all over with black and brown : the feathers on the lower part of the neck, breast, and shoulders, look like scales, beautifully margined and crossed with curved black and white lines : those of the back, scapulars, and sides, are light brown, marked transversely with nar- rower waved dusky streaks : the belly and thighs are dingy white, more or less sprinkled with grey : the lower part of the back dark brown : rump and vent black ; and the tail ash, edged with white. The ridge

and lesser coverts of the wings are of a pale rufous
brown, crossed obliquely by the beauty spot, which is
a tri-coloured bar of purplish red, white, and black :
the greater quills are dusky : legs orange red. The
wings of the female are barred like those of the male,
but the colours are of a much duller cast, and her
breast, instead of his beautiful markings, is only plain
brown, spotted with black.

Birds of this species breed in the desert marshes of
the north, and remain there throughout the spring and
summer. On the approach of winter they leave the
European and Siberian parts of Russia, Sweden, &c.
and commonly make their appearance about the month
of November, on the French, British, and other more
southern shores, where they remain till the end of
February, and then return to their northern haunts.
They are very shy and wary birds, feeding only in the
night, and lurking concealed among the rushes in the
watery waste during the day, in which they are seldom
seen on the wing.

These birds shew themselves expert in diving as well
as in swimming, and often disappoint the sportsman in
his aim ; for the instant they see the flash of the pan,
they disappear, and dive to a distant secure retreat.
The foregoing figure was made from a Wycliffe specimen now in the Newcastle Museum.

THE POCHARD.

POKER, DUNBIRD, OR GREAT-HEADED WIGEON.

(Anas ferina, Linn.—*Le Canard Milouin,* Buff.)

THE Pochard is nineteen inches in length, and two feet and a half in breadth, and weighs about one pound thirteen ounces. The bill is of a dark lead coloured grey, with the tip and sides near the nostrils, black: irides fine deep yellow. The head and neck are of a glossy chesnut, joined to a large space of sooty black which covers the breast, and is spread over the shoulders: the lower part of the back, the rump, tail coverts, and vent, are also black: the rest of the plumage, both above and below, is wholly covered with prettily freckled slender dusky threads, disposed transversely in close-set zigzag lines, on a pale ground, more or less shaded off with ash and brown. The primary quills are brown, with dusky tips; the secondaries lead grey, tinged with brown, and slightly tipped with dull white. The tail consists of twelve short feathers, of a dark brownish ash, which have also a hoary grey appearance : the legs and toes are lead colour, shaded and dashed with black.

This species is without the beauty-spot on the wings, and has altogether a more plain grave looking plumage than others of this tribe. The specimen from which the above figure was drawn, was shot at Axwell Park, in the county of Durham : the description was taken from one shot in January, near Holy Island. The former differed from the latter in wanting the black on the rump and vent, and in some other slight variations in the shadings of its colours.

" The head of the female is of a pale reddish brown: the breast is of rather a deeper colour: the coverts of the wings plain ash colour: the back marked like that of the male: the belly ash coloured."*

These birds leave the north on the approach of winter, and migrate southward as far, it is said, as Egypt, in Africa, and Carolina and Louisiana, in America. They arrive in the marshes of France about the end of October, in tolerably numerous flocks; and considerable numbers of them are caught in the fens of Lincolnshire during the winter season, and sold in the London markets, where they and the female Wigeons are indiscriminately called Dunbirds, and are esteemed excellent eating. It has not yet been discovered whether any of them remain to breed in England.

The Pochard is of a plump round shape, and its walk is heavy, ungraceful and waddling; but when on the wing, they fly with greater rapidity than the Mallard, and in flocks of from twenty to forty, commonly in a close compact body, whereby they may be easily

* Pennant.

distinguished from the triangular shaped flocks of the Wild Duck, as well as by the difference of the noise of their wings.

The few attempts which have been hitherto made to domesticate this species have failed of success. They do pretty well where they have plenty of water, but it is said that they cannot bear walking about on hard pebbly ground.

THE PINTAIL DUCK.

SEA PHEASANT, CRACKER, OR WINTER DUCK.

(Anas acuta, Linn.—*Le Canard à longue queue,* Buff.)

THIS handsome-looking bird is twenty-eight inches
in length, and thirty-eight in breadth, and weighs
about twenty-four ounces.   The bill is rather long,
black in the middle, and blue on the edges: the irides
reddish: the head and throat are of a rusty brown,
mottled with small dark spots, and tinged behind the
ears with purple: the nape and upper part of the neck
are dusky, margined by a narrow white line, which
runs down on each side, and falling into a broader
stripe of the same colour, extends itself on the fore
part as far as the breast; the rest of the neck, the
breast, and the upper part of the back, are elegantly

penciled with black and white waved lines: the lower
back and sides of the body are undulated in the same
manner, but with lines more freckled, less distinct, and
paler: the scapulars are long and pointed, each feather
black down the middle, with white edges: the coverts
of the wings are ash brown, tipped with dull orange:
below these the wing is obliquely crossed by the beauty
spot of glossy bronze purple green, with a lower border
of black and white: this spangle is formed by the outer
webs and tips of the middle quills: the rest of the quills
are dusky.   All the tail feathers are of a brown ash colour, with pale edges, except the two middle ones, which
are black, slightly glossed with green, considerably
longer than the others, and end in a point: the belly
and the sides of the vent are white:* under tail coverts
black: legs and feet small, and of a lead colour.   The
female is less than the male, and her plumage is of a
much plainer cast, all the upper parts being brown, with
each feather margined more or less with white, inclining to red or yellow: the greater coverts and secondary
quills are tipped with cream colour and white, which
form a bar across the wings.   The fore part of the neck,
the breast, and the belly, to the vent, are of a dull white,
obscurely spotted with brown.   The tail is long and
pointed, but the two middle feathers do not extend
themselves beyond the rest, like those of the male.

These birds do not visit the temperate and warm climates in great numbers, except in very severe winters,
the great bulk of them dropping short, and remaining
during that season in various parts of the Russian do-

* In some, the belly and fore part of the neck are of a reddish buff,
or cream colour.

minions, Sweden, Norway, &c. and also in the same latitudes in both Asia and America. They are seldom
numerous in England, but flocks of them are sometimes
abundantly spread along the isles and shores of Scotland and Ireland, and on the interior lakes of both
countries, as well as those of the continent, as far south
as Italy, and in America, as far south as New York.
They are esteemed excellent eating.

The Pintail Duck is of a taller or more lengthened
shape than any of the other species, and in the opinion
of the Count de Buffon, seems to form the link between
the Duck and the Garganey.

THE TUFTED DUCK.*

(Anas fuligula, Linn.—*Le petit Morillon,* Brisson.)

THIS is a plump, round, and short-shaped species.
The male is distinguished by a pendent crest, overhanging the nape of the neck, two inches in length.
The weight is about two pounds, length eighteen inches.
The bill is broad, of a dark lead colour; the nail black:
irides deep orange : the head is black, glossed with
purple : the neck, breast, and all the upper parts, are
of a deep brown or black : the scapulars faintly pow-
dered or sprinkled with light spots, so minute as not to
be observed at a short distance.   The wings are crossed
by a narrow white bar : the belly, sides, and under coverts of the wings, are of a pure white : the vent white,

---

* The tuft is sometimes wanting, and in that state has been made
a distinct species. *Montagu.*

mixed with dusky. The tail consists of fourteen very short feathers : the legs are of a dark lead colour ; webs black. The female is of a browner colour than the male, and has no crest.

The habits, manners, and haunts of this species are much the same as those of the Golden-Eye, and they return northward about the same time. Latham says " the French allow these birds to be eaten on maigre days and in lent; as they do also the Scoter: but though the flesh of the latter is now and then tolerable, that of the tufted Duck is seldom otherwise than excellent."

THE TEAL.

(Anas Crecca, Linn.—*La petite Sarcelle.)*

THIS beautiful little Duck seldom exceeds eleven
ounces in weight, or measures more, stretched out, than
fourteen inches and a half in length, and twenty-three
and a half in breadth.   The bill is a dark lead colour,
tipped with black: irides pale hazel: a glossy bottle-
green patch, edged on the upper side with pale brown,
and beneath with cream-coloured white, covers each
eye, and extends to the nape of the neck: the rest of
the head,* and the upper part of the neck, are of a deep
reddish chesnut, darkest on the forehead, and freckled
on the chin and about the eyes with cream-coloured
spots: the hinder part of the neck, the shoulders, part
of the scapulars, sides under the wings, and lower belly,

* In some of this species the feathers on the head are lengthened
out into a crest; the upper part of which is pale brown, the under
deep purple.

towards the vent, are elegantly penciled with black, ash-
brown, and white transverse waved lines: the breast,
greatly resembling the beautifully spotted appearance
of an Indian shell, is of a pale brown or reddish yellow,
and each feather is tipped with a roundish heart-shaped
black spot: the belly is a cream-coloured white: back
and rump ash-brown, each feather freckled and edged
with a paler colour: vent black: the primary quills, and
lesser and greater coverts, are brown; the last deeply
tipped with white, which forms a bar across the wings:
the first six of the secondary quills are of a fine velvet
black; those next to them, towards the scapulars, are
of a most resplendent glossy green, and both are tipped
with white, forming the divided black and green bar, or
beauty-spot of the wings. The tail consists of fourteen
feathers, of a hoary brown colour, with pale edges: the
legs and feet are of a dirty lead colour. The female,
which is less than the male, is prettily freckled about
the head and neck with brown and white. She has
not the green patch behind the eyes, but a brown
streak there, which extends itself to the nape of the
neck: the crown of the head is dark brown: the upper
mandible yellow on the edges, olive green on the sides,
and olive brown on the ridge; nail black, and the under bill yellow: breast, belly, and vent glossy yellowish
white, spotted on the latter parts with brown: the upper plumage is dark brown, each feather bordered with
rusty brown, and edged with grey: the wings and legs
nearly the same as those of the male.

The Teal is common in England in the winter
months, but it is uncertain whether or not they remain

throughout the year to breed,* as is the case in France. The female makes a large nest, composed of soft dried grasses, (and, it is said, the pith of rushes) lined with feathers, and cunningly concealed in a hole among the roots of reeds and bulrushes, near the edge of the water; and some assert that it rests on the surface of the water so as to rise and fall with it. The eggs are of the size of those of a Pigeon, six or seven in number, and of a dull white colour, marked with small brownish spots; but it appears that they sometimes lay ten or twelve eggs, for Buffon remarks that that number of young are seen in clusters on the pools, feeding on cresses, wild chervil, &c. and no doubt, as they grow up, they feed like other Ducks, on the various seeds, grasses, and water plants, as well as upon the smaller animated beings with which all stagnant waters are so abundantly stored. The Teal is highly esteemed for the excellent flavour of its flesh.

* Dr Heysham says, " the Teal is now known to breed in the mosses about Carlisle."

THE SHAG.

SKART, SCARFE, OR GREEN CORMORANT.

(Pelecanus graculus, Linn.—*Le petit Cormoran, ou le Nigaud,* Buff.)*

THE form, the aspect altogether, the outward conformation of all the parts, the character, manners and habits, and the places of abode, of this species, are nearly like those of the Cormorant; but they do not associate, and these make their nests on the rugged shelvy sides and crevices of the rocky precipices or projecting cliffs which overhang the sea, while the others make theirs on the summits above them; and these are at once distinguished from the others by the

greenness of the upper, and brownness of the under
plumage, and also in being of a much less size; the
largest Shags weighing only about four pounds, and
measuring nearly two feet six inches in length, and
three feet eight in breadth.   The bill is of a more slender make, but nearly as long as that of the Cormorant;
the head, in the male, is crested in the same manner;
the middle claw is serrated; and its tail, consisting of
twelve stiff feathers stained with green, is also of the
same form, and hoary or dirty appearance, as that of the
Cormorant: the crown of the head, hinder part of the
neck, lower back, and rump, are of a plain black, or
very dark green, shining like satin: the upper back, or
shoulders, together with the scapulars and wings, are
nearly of the same colour, but with a tinge of bronze
brown, and each feather is distinctly edged with purple
glossed black: the under parts are clouded with dusky
dirty white and brown.

The Shag is as greedy and voracious as the Cormorant, and like that bird, after having over-gorged its
stomach, is often found on shore in a sleepy or stupified
state; but when this torpor is over, and they appear
again upon the water, they are then extremely alert,
and are not easily shot, for both kinds dive the instant
they see the flash of the gun, and take care afterwards
to keep out of its reach.   In swimming they carry their
head very erect, while the body seems nearly sub-
merged, and from their feathers not being quite impervious to the water, they do not remain very long upon
it at a time, but are frequently seen flying about, or
sitting on the rocks, flapping the moisture from their
wings, or keeping them for some time expanded, to dry

in the sun and the wind. Nothwithstanding the strong
and offensive smell emitted from the Shags and the Cor-
morants, some instances are not wanting of their having
been eaten in this country; but before they are cooked,
they must undergo a certain sweetening process, part of
which consists in their being first skinned and drawn,
and then wrapped up in a clean cloth, and buried for
some time in the earth; after which they are made ready for eating in various ways, though generally potted
like Moor Game.

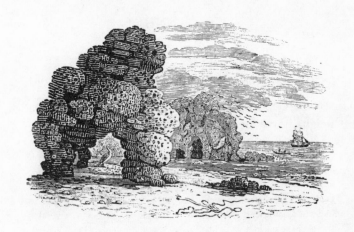

THE GANNET,*

GAN, SOLAND OR SOLAN GOOSE.

(Pelecanus Bassanus, Linn.—*Le Fou de Bassan,* Buff.)

THE Gannet is generally about seven pounds in weight, three feet in length, and six in breadth. The

* This bird is essentially different from the Cormorant. The great length of the wings, in proportion to the tail; the striking difference in the shape of the bill; the impossibility of diving, except for a moment, and that from the wing, and never from the water, appear to indicate a sufficient difference to authorize a new genus, and later writers have made it so. The base of the bill is dentated and jointed, which admits considerable motion of the upper mandible; there is no pouch like the Pelican. It is, strictly speaking, an oceanic bird. The Cormorant is the reverse, being a shore bird, and much on the rocks as well as in the water. " The singular communication between the

bill is of a pale or lead-coloured blue, six inches long,
a little jagged on the edges, strong and straight to the
tip, which is inclined a little downwards: the upper
bill is furnished with a distinct rib or ridge, running
along from the tip nearly to its base, on each side of
which it is furrowed, without any visible appearance of
nostrils: the tongue is small, and placed far within
the mouth, all the inside of which is black: a darkish
line passes from the brow over the eyes, which are
surrounded with a naked blue skin, and, like those of
the Owl, are set in the head so as to look nearly
straight forward, and the extreme paleness of the
irides gives them a keen wild stare. The gape of the
mouth is very wide, and seems more lengthened, by a
slip of naked black skin, which is extended on each
side from the corners beyond the cheeks: these features of its countenance, altogether, give it somewhat
the appearance of wearing spectacles. A loose black
bare dilatable skin, capable of great distension, hung
from the blades of the under bill, and extended over
the throat, serves it as a pouch to carry provisions to
its mate, or its young. The body is flat and well
cloathed with feathers; the neck long: the crown of
the head, nape, and, in some specimens, the hinder
part of the neck, are of a buff colour; greater quills
and bastard wings black, and the rest of the plumage
white. The tail is wedge-shaped, and consists of

lungs and cellular membrane, which enables it to contain three full
inspirations of the human lungs, subject to the will of the bird; and
the cellular membrane being the breeding place of an apterous insect," Montagu seems to consider as peculiar to the internal conformation of this bird. The trachea in both sexes resembles that of the
Cormorant.

twelve tapering sharp-pointed feathers, the middle ones the longest. The legs and feet are nearly of the same colour and conformation as those of the Cormorant, but they are curiously marked by three pea-green stripes, which run down each leg, and branch off along the toes. The male and female are nearly alike, but the young birds, during the first year, appear as if they were of a distinct species, for their plumage is then of a dusky colour, speckled all over with triangular white spots.

They make their nest in the caverns and fissures, or on the ledges of the louring precipice, as well as on the plain surface of the ground : it is formed of a great quantity of withered grasses and sea-weeds of various kinds, gathered with much labour from the barren soil, or picked up floating about upon the water. The female lays three white eggs, somewhat less than those of a Goose, although ornithologists assert that she will lay only one egg, if left to herself undisturbed, and that when this egg is taken away she then lays a second, and in like manner a third, which she is generally permitted to hatch, and rear the young one.*   " The male and female hatch and fish by turns; the fisher

* " The Solan Geese have always some of their number that keep watch in the night time, and if the centinel is surprised, (as it often happens) all that flock are taken, one after another; but if the centinel be awake at the approach of the creeping fowlers, and hear a noise, he cries softly *Grog, Grog,* at which the flock do not move ; but if this centinel see or hear the fowler approaching, he cries softly *Bir, Bir,* which would seem to import danger, since immediately after, all the tribe take wing, leaving the disappointed fowlers without any prospect of success for that night."—*Martin.*

returns to the nest with five or six herrings in its gorget, all entire and undigested, which the hatcher pulls out from the throat of its provider, and swallows them, making at the same time a loud noise."

These birds are common on the coasts of Norway and Iceland, and are said to be met with in great numbers about New Holland and New Zealand; they breed also on the coasts of Newfoundland, and migrate southward along the American shores as far as South Carolina: they are noticed, indeed, by navigators, as being met with, dispersed over both hemispheres, and are probably one great family spread over the whole globe; but their greatest known rendezvous is the Hebrides and other solitary rocky isles of North Britain, where their nests, in the months of May and June, are described as so closely placed together, that it is difficult to walk without treading upon some of them; and it is said that the swarms of the old birds are so prodigious, that when they rise into the air, they stun the ear with their noise, and over-shadow the ground like the clouds.* Besides the small isle of Borea, and St Kilda, noticed by Martin, Pennant and other writers mention the isle of Ailsa, in the Frith of Clyde; the Stack of Souliskerry, near the Orkneys; the Skellig Isles, off the coast of Kerry, Ireland; and the Bass Isle, in the Frith of Forth. This last-men-

---

* Martin, in his History of and Voyage to St Kilda, published in 1698, says, " the inhabitants of St Kilda take their measures from the flight of these fowls, when the heavens are not clear, as from a sure compass, experience shewing that every tribe of fowls bend their course to their respective quarters, though out of sight of the isle; this appeared clearly in our gradual advances; and their motion being compared, did exactly quadrate with our compass."

tioned isle is farmed out at a considerable rent, for
the eggs of the various kinds of water fowl with which
it swarms; and the produce of the Solan Geese forms
a large portion of this rent; for great numbers of their
young ones are taken every season, and sold in Edin-
burgh, where they are esteemed a favourite dish, being
generally roasted, and eaten before dinner.   On the
other bleak and bare isles, the inhabitants, during a
great part of the year, depend for their support upon
these birds and their eggs, which are taken in amazing
numbers, and are the principal articles of their food.*
From the nests placed upon the ground the eggs are
easily picked up one after another, in great numbers,
as fast as they are laid; but in robbing the nests built
in the precipices, chiefly for the sake of the birds, the
business wears a very different aspect: there, before
the dearly earned booty can be secured, the adventur-
ous fowler, trained to it from his youth, and familiarised to the danger, must first approach the brow of the
fearful precipice, to view and to trace his progress on
the broken pendent rocks beneath him: over these rocks,
which (perhaps a hundred fathoms lower) are dashed
by the foaming surge, he is from a prodigious height
about to be suspended.   After addressing himself in
prayer to the Supreme Disposer of events, with a mind
prepared for the arduous task, he is let down by a
rope, either held fast by his comrades, or fixed into

* They preserve the eggs in stone huts or pyramids, which they
build for that purpose, as well as for a shelter to the fowlers : in these
pyramids they cover up the eggs with turf ashes, which defend them
from the air, dryness being their only preservative, and moisture
their corruption : by this method, it is said, they keep them fresh and
fit for use, for six, seven, or even for eight months."—*Martin.*

the ground on the summit, with his signal cord, his
pole-net, his pole-hook, &c. and thus equipped, he is
enabled in his progress, either to stop, to ascend, or
descend, as he sees occasion. Somtimes by swinging
himself from one ledge to another, with the help of his
hook, he mounts upwards, and clambers from place to
place; and, at other opportunities, by springing backwards, he can dart himself into the hollow caverns of
the projecting rock, which he commonly finds well
stored with the objects of his pursuit, whence the plunder, chiefly consisting of the full-grown young birds,
is drawn up to the top, or tossed down to the boat at
the bottom, according to the situation of concurring
circumstances of time and place. In these hollows he
takes his rest, and sometimes remains during the night,
especially when they happen to be at such vast and
stupendous heights. To others of less magnitude the
fowlers commonly climb from the bottom, with the
help of their hooked poles only, by which they assist,
and push or pull up each other from hold to hold, and
in this manner traverse the whole front of the frightful
scar. To a feeling mind the very sight of this hazard-
ous employment, in whatever way it is pursued, is
painful; for, indeed, it often happens that these ad-
venturous poor men, in this mode of obtaining their
living, slip their hold, are precipitated from one projection to another, with increasing velocity, and fall
mangled upon the rocks, or are for ever buried in the
abyss beneath.

THE SCOLOPAX SABINI.

THE bill, from the tip to the brow, is about two inches
and five eighths long: the whole plumage is composed
of black, brown, and ferruginous; each feather tipped,
edged, spotted and crossed with the latter colour,
which predominates on the cheeks, neck, and upper
part of the breast; on the sides of the head the feathers
are also very slightly fringed in small dots of that colour; the ears are nearly on a line with the corners of
the mouth: in this respect, as well as in the general
contour of its figure, it bears a resemblance to the
Woodcock, but its bill is much longer in proportion
to the size of the bird. It is feathered nearly to the
knees; the legs short, toes long, and without any connecting web or membrane between them: they appear
to be of a dusky or dark green colour. The author
was favoured by N. A. Vigors, Esq. with a preserved

specimen, from which the above figure is taken. The bird was shot near Old Glass, Queen's County, Ireland, on the 21st August, 1822.

A female of this species was shot on the banks of the Medway, near Rochester, on the 26th October, 1824, exactly resembling this specimen except in being somewhat smaller.

THE SELNINGER SANDPIPER.

(Tringa Maritima, Brun :—*Le Chevalier rayè,* Buff.)

THE base of the bill is reddish; the rest of it to the
tip black; the head and neck are dusky brown, tinged
with ash, and somewhat clouded on the latter; the
side of the brow, a little before the eye, is marked with
a whitish spot; the chin and gullet are white; on the
upper part of the breast the feathers are dusky, like
the neck, and fringed with white, but they appear
grey: the lesser coverts of the wings the same, but
much darker in the middle, and much lighter on the
edges: the back, scapulars, secondaries, and tertials,
are deepish brown, more or less bronzed and edged
with dull grey; and the latter and secondaries are
edged and tipped with white; the quills are deep
dusky brown, very narrowly edged with dull white;
the tail is also the same, with the edges of the two

outside feathers white; the under parts are white, spotted on the sides to the tail, with dull brown; the legs are yellow, short, and like the Knot's, are feathered to the knees.

This Sandpiper seems, from its resemblance to the Knot, to bear a strong affinity or relationship to a family of that species. Latham gives, under the above name, a short and imperfect account of it. He says, it inhabits Norway and Iceland, lives about the sea shore, and emits a piping note. Montagu also does not seem to know much of its history; he calls it the Purple Sandpiper, and makes it the Tringa nigricans of the Linnæan Transactions, and also the Striated Sandpiper of the Arctic Zoology, and gives synonymes of other authors. He does not say why it has been called the Purple Sandpiper, and in the above specimen, it has not a shade of that colour on its plumage. This bird, an old male, was shot near Yarmouth, and the preserved specimen was lent to this work by Mr Yarrel, to whom we beg our acknowledgements.